Happy Habits is a practical actionabl(...) on a journey of habit transformation.

When reading this book, you will find everything you need to change your habits and be able to do it right away.

I highly recommend *Happy Habits* because I know it will help you in life and work.

J.R. Heimbigner
The Minimalist Author, Writer and Content Creator
(Spokane, WA)
www.substack.com/@jrheimbigner

Having known Gunnar for years, I've been fortunate to witness the depth of his thinking on social selling, networking, and intentional creativity.

Happy Habits is not just another guide; it is a deeply considered blueprint for those navigating change, rebuilding rhythm, or seeking clarity in uncertain times. Each chapter meets you with both honesty and practicality, offering steps that are not only doable but also refreshingly introspective.

This book does not overwhelm; it anchors. In many ways, it reads like a culmination of Gunnar's personal evolution, an almost eponymous reflection of the habits, values, and remarkable resilience he has lived, taught, and consistently modelled for years.

Cybill Getgood
Co-Founder of The People Avenue (Adelaide)
www.linkedin.com/in/cybillgetgood

In *Happy Habits* Gunnar focuses on habits, not so much for productivity as for a better life.

This book brings together valuable ideas into a comprehensive, practical guidebook on developing and achieving great habits. The ideas are explained with personal examples that show clearly what works and why they work.

As a leader focused on personal growth and development, I know how important habits are. I especially appreciate the practical questions and next steps scattered throughout the book and will be applying the 4P Framework into my own life.

Harley Hochstetler

Executive Director at Nielsen (Sydney)
www.linkedin.com/in/harleyhoch

Your book *Happy Habits* arrived at a perfect time, just as I left the corporate world to pursue freelance writing full-time.

I truly loved your book. It's filled with gold nuggets of wisdom and wonderful suggestions drawn from your personal experiences. Each section is clearly written, and the exercises at the end are especially valuable in helping the readers put their learning into action.

Happy Habits is a must-read book for anyone looking to create a more fulfilling life and to navigate any transition with success.

Sal Gallaher

Author and Freelance Writer (Sydney)
www.linkedin.com/in/sal-gallaher

Happy Habits doesn't push productivity, it invites reflection. Gunnar's words feel like a deep breath, offering space to rethink what's driving you and why.

Through personal stories and grounded examples, he guides you gently back to yourself. The habits shares aren't rigid, they're thoughtful, flexible, and surprisingly doable.

This book reminded me that progress can start with small shifts in awareness. If you've been feeling stuck, this is the kind of book that quietly changes things.

Dimka Dimitrova

Marketing Automation Consultant (London)
www.linkedin.com/in/dimkadimitrova

A good habit enriches life; a bad habit limits it. In his book *Happy Habits*, Gunnar shares practical tools and insights gathered from years of learning and personal practice, so he could pass them on to you.

This book is a gift for anyone ready to improve life's quality by nurturing new habits. I recommend setting aside quiet time for reflection and journaling, using the questions at each chapter's end.

Nothing comes by accident. If you've found this book, perhaps it's meant to serve you now.

Eleen Yaw

Life Coach & Happiness Coach (Sydney)
www.linkedin.com/in/eleenyaw

As someone with late-diagnosed ADHD, I am often looking for ways to make my life more manageable and productive.

Having read other books on the subject of habits, I can say that Gunnar has taken a unique approach with fresh – and indeed, happy – ideas for methods to get into good habits in our life, and the exercises at the end of each part are easily manageable.

The part that stood out for me the most was the Partner section (Part Four), which has reminded me to engage with others in my goal of becoming more organised.

I applaud Gunnar on this book and give it my full recommendation for those needing to get a handle on a busy or chaotic life.

Fleur Hull
Marketing Coach, Author of "Career after COVID-19" (Perth)
www.linkedin.com/in/fleurhull

A smashing hit in the world of habits. No exaggeration.

This book is an effective compass for those bogged down with setbacks in life who don't know how to press the reset button after. It shows a way to adopt new habits, sure. But it also tells you how to resume after a break, minus the stress and a sense of failure.

This book shows the perfect way to make personal growth more fun, easy, and sustainable. A perfect combination of philosophy and action points, the one I've never seen anywhere else.

Tanvee Dharmadhikari
Dentist and Content Creator (Mumbai)
www.linkedin.com/in/tanvdentwriter

As someone whose research and life's work revolve around the science and practice of habits, *Happy Habits* offered me a fresh and valuable perspective.

It is engaging and insightful, drawing from the author's inspiring transition from a challenging life chapter to a state of fulfilment and joy. The 4P Model of *Happy Habits* is clearly and thoughtfully articulated, providing readers with practical, sustainable strategies to build habits grounded in awareness, purpose, and action.

This is am empowering book that can truly enrich the lives of those ready to create lasting positive change.

Dr. Mehmet Yildiz
Cognitive Scientist and Author of 50+ books (Melbourne)
www.linkedin.com/in/mehmetyildiz

Habits are powerful because they remove daily decision fatigue – small actions with massive impact. That's exactly what Gunnar highlights.

But more than that, he shows how to weave habits naturally into your lifestyle, not treat them like rigid systems. His refreshingly reversed approach isn't about discipline; it's about ease, flow, and real-life success.

Katja Groesser
Clever Finance Girls (Antalya)
www.cleverfinancegirls.com

I just finished reading Happy Habitz and I've gotta tell you, I read the whole thing in one sitting... in my hammock.

And honestly, with a name like Gunnar Habit(Z), it was kinda inevitable that he'd write a book about habits someday, right? :)

Here's what makes this book fun: Gunnar picks out the best and most powerful quotes from giants like James Clear, the stuff you see on every beach or holiday bookshelf, and then he adds his own "two cents," expands on them, and makes you think about habits in a new way.

It's super light, super easy to read, and honestly, pretty entertaining. I'd even call it a happy read. You enjoy it. What really stuck with me: you can CREATE habits and put yourself in a position of luck. You can start (or stop!) right now.

Habits don't have to be overwhelming. They can be tiny micro-steps that stack up over time. Apparently, I'm not a strict daily writer, but I'm in an (almost) daily writer habit. I write whenever I find the time, and that consistency adds up.

I think it's wild that Gunnar wrote this book in the cracks of time, alongside his day job, while also posting almost daily on LinkedIn and Substack. He's living proof that writing in public itself can become a habit.

So if you've been waiting for a sign to finally kickstart — or kill off — some habits, this is it. No excuses. Grab *Happy Habits*, read it, and start building those micro-steps today. Bravo, Gunnar!

Kristina God
Founder of Online Writing Club on Substack (Bad Homburg)
www.onlinewritingclub.com

HAPPY HABITS

Feel Better. Focus Better. Live Better.
One Habit at a Time.

Gunnar Habitz

Edited by Belle van den Hout (Sydney)
Cover design by the author with ideas from his Substack community
Images by Canva

ISBN: 978-1-7638207-4-6 (Paperback)
ISBN: 978-1-7638207-5-3 (eBook)
ISBN: 978-1-7638207-6-0 (Audiobook)
First published in Australia in 2025

Acknowledgement

On a relaxed Easter Saturday evening I sat on a bench at Coogee Beach in Sydney's Eastern suburbs. The atmosphere was filled with good vibes and laughter, the right place to read a book on my Kindle.

I picked "Discipline" by J.R. Heimbigner, a great book to read in contrary to the relaxed environment. Coming to Australia from Germany and Switzerland, the title resonated well with me.

After a few pages, I reflected about J.R.'s approach of writing so-called "mini books"; that means those with up to 100-120 pages or less than 20,000 words. Books that cover one topic towards one transformation, not ground-breaking Pulitzer price candidates.

In comparison, my first English business book, *Connect & Act – Systematic Social Selling*, sports 42,000 words across 160 pages with a range of experts who shared their wisdom.

Writing *Happy Habits* as the starting point of a new series was a pleasure, especially as I wrote most part of it in parallel to my next business book, *LinkedIn for Startups*.

I would like to thank those who actively contributed to this project, such as Natalie Tran for the foreword, the four expert voices Rachel WingMan, Sophie Anderson, Lloyd Thompson, and Frederik Böhnke, as well as editor Belle van den Hout for turning my words into proper English.

No book shall be written without a community built prior to that. At this stage I would like to acknowledge my networks on LinkedIn and especially on Substack who supported this project by cheering from the side lines, adding invaluable pieces, and providing ongoing feedback.

The content of this book also turned into my new online course program with a totally different concept than from my earlier courses thanks to the example of Veronica Llorca-Smith's highly recommended Substack course.

This book and those I published before would have been impossible to write without the ongoing support of my wife Alexandra – my personal coach, hardest critic and best friend of more than 27 years!

Gunnar

Foreword

We are the sum of our habits. Many of us know this phrase. I often share it with my clients too – whether we realise it or not, the life we live today is shaped by the choices we've put on autopilot.

The next question to ask is "Are those choices aligned with the life I want to live?"

I learnt early in my coaching days that transformation isn't achieved by one grand or intense action but built in the everyday. I saw over and over again that it takes a moment of clarity, a shift in mindset, and quiet small but powerful habits repeated with intention.

I would first invite my clients to pause. To take stock of everything. To examine what's running in the background of their daily life (without judgment) and to ask, "Is this still serving me?" Many of us often default to survival mode, especially when things get tough. This is what I call "reactive push" energy.

Real change happens when we create space internally (to listen to ourselves inwardly); this requires slowing down to reflect. We can then work out what we need and redesign our habits to support the version of ourselves we're becoming. This is when we can speed up. That is why I love this phrase "Internal stillness, external speed".

In our many discussions, Gunnar and I have also talked about what it takes to achieve transformation. We discussed productivity, presence, energy, and alignment and always come back to how simple, joyful shifts performed daily and embedded in our daily lives can create profound transformation. Daily walks and movement, daily writing, blocking out focus time... all that helps us reclaim our days, rewire our thinking, and reconnect with what matters.

I am so excited for these pages ahead which Gunnar has penned and will leave you with a couple of reminders: Stop and honestly reflect, play with the practices and experiment with what feels good to you and what works for you. The small things you do daily can build the big life you desire.

With purpose,

Natalie Tran
Transition With Purpose

Natalie Tran
Transition & Business Coach, Executive Coaching,
Host of the Transition with Purpose Podcast
www.linkedin.com/in/natalie-tran-coach-melbourne

Contents

Welcome

*"Motivation is what gets you started.
Habit is what keeps you going."*

Jim Rohn

Dear reader,

Welcome to my book *Happy Habits*! Please allow me a quick intro and tell you a little bit about how this book came about.

When I started learning English in primary school next to Latin, I found out that this word "habit" is included in my last name – just we write it with a "z" at the end.

And when I started writing articles and books, I knew that there will be a dedicated piece about it. It took me half of a lifetime to have enough experience that I'm ready to share something about building good habits or reducing bad ones.

The tune for this book might be the song "Hard Habit to Break" from rock band Chicago – a classic song I often listened to when learning English in high school.

I found an important principle when I worked as software engineer in the automotive industry: the power of choice.

Applying that to the hospitality industry, the boring question "Do you want a dessert" could be replaced with "We have a tasty tiramisu or refreshing sorbet – which one do you prefer for your dessert?" The theoretical option of ordering nothing verbally disappeared.

Transitioning that example, I won't just ask you "Do you want to build better habits?"

Instead, the motivating question should be this one: "Would you like to feel more focused, more connected, or more in control of your energy – starting this week?"

I had a dream of writing a book about habits for a long time. But I didn't set out to write this book from a place of control.

In fact, it started with a disruption, even three of them. The first was a corporate layoff in Switzerland. I had worked hard for 16 years, contributed deeply to the company, and suddenly... it was over. This moment forced me to pause not just in terms of career but emotionally and mentally.

That pause eventually led me to move down under to Sydney, Australia where I started from scratch – building a new life, finding a new rhythm and building a new network.

Later down the track I faced two more layoffs: one from Hootsuite after 2.5 years and another from GoTo after just nine months. However, by the time of the third disruption, I had something well developed which I didn't have before:

Habits.

One habit helped me in particular: I posted on LinkedIn every week using the same hashtag, #socialsellingmonday. *Every single week* since November 2018 without fail! Well, not always on a Monday, mostly on the Australian Tuesday which is the American Monday.

At the time of writing this, I posted various thoughts about my favourite topic Social Selling for about 333 weeks in a row. That's more than six years of consistent content.

No excuses. No perfect conditions. Not polished. Just rhythm. And what did that habit do?

- It led to writing my first business book in English, *Connect & Act*
- Which led to visibility through my birthday book launch
- Which led to consulting work to the value of 30X more than book royalties

In short: I didn't panic. I posted.

When things get messy, systems and habits save you, and that is the heart of habit-building which I will talk about in this book. It might be different than most other books you read about this topic.

Most other books about habits typically begin with habits. This one doesn't. Instead, I want to challenge you to start from the end. Imagine your future self. What would you like to feel more of?

- Focus?
- Confidence?
- Calm?
- Momentum?

Now let's work that backwards:

- What kind of person consistently feels that way?
- What simple system supports that identity?
- What habit could be the anchor for that system?

That is reverse engineering. In other words: it is about writing your life forward by looking backward.

This book is not a lecture. It's a toolkit. You will walk through four simple but powerful stages which I call the **4P Framework**:

1. **Pause** – Recognise the moment that calls for change.
2. **Plan** – Design habits that align with your personal values.
3. **Practice** – Build consistency, even when motivation fades.
4. **Partner** – Create support systems so habits can thrive.

Therefore, here's your first habit: **Choose your focus**. Pick the area where you would like to feel just a little better. Then head to chapter one and take the first step. Because you don't need to change everything.

Just one habit – at a time.

Part 1 – Pause

"Once you understand that habits can change, you have the freedom – and the responsibility – to remake them."

Charles Duhigg

Recognise the Moment That Calls for Change

Welcome to the first part of this book where I would like to introduce the concept of pausing before an attempt to develop good habits or reduce those bad ones.

As a reflective pause is an underrated method in rhetoric in our noisy world, we need to pause for a reflection about the little things we do.

I found inspiration for this first part in the famous book *The Power of Habit* from the American journalist Charles Duhigg. It explores the science behind why habits form, how they operate, and how they can be changed.

At the heart of Duhigg's model is the so-called "habit loop" – a cycle consisting of cue, routine, and reward. They represent the trigger, the behaviour, and the benefit. The cover shows a friendly rat who decided to escape that "rat race" or "hamster wheel" loop.

This neurological loop drives everything from personal routines to corporate success stories, and even societal shifts. By understanding how to isolate each element, individuals and organisations can reshape their behaviours to support more desirable outcomes.

The author illustrates his insights with an impressive range of real-world examples, including how Starbucks trains their employees to respond habitually to customer complaints, how Olympic swimmer Michael Phelps mentally rehearsed his personal victories, and how the organisation Alcoholics Anonymous rewires destructive patterns through belief and community.

The book also explores the concept of "keystone habits": these are certain behaviours that, once changed, can trigger widespread transformation across other areas of life.

Ultimately, *The Power of Habit* reveals that change doesn't just happen overnight, but it happens through intentional effort and awareness. Habits aren't the destiny, instead they are systems that can be reshaped.

Released in 2012, the book has become a modern classic in behavioural science and self-improvement literature. It bridged the gap between academic research and everyday relevance, becoming a foundational text in modern habit theory. Despite being published more than a decade ago it still reads like written for present times.

One of Duhigg's core insights is that before you can change a habit, you must first identify it. In other words: You must press pause long enough to notice the mentioned loop.

In *Happy Habits* this first step is **Pause**. It is the space where you observe what is driving your behaviours and begin to break free from automatic responses. Just as Duhigg shows that "keystone habits" unlock broader change, this section invites you to reflect on the moments that shook up your routines and to use that disruption as an invitation to redesign your life.

The key question here: what drives this Pause moment? Can we plan that? Does it come over night as an epiphany to know the right moment?

This Pause moment often arrives out of the blue as an unwanted event which the Canadian coach Dennis Geelen calls a "Happy Accident". In his remarkable parable book, *The Accidental Solopreneur*, he shared how an unwanted layoff became the disruptive power of the protagonist to pause, reflect and develop new habits.

This is exactly what happened to me as well in October 2015 when my former manager told me that my journey in the company was over after 16 years of constant service and well-planned career progression.

I took that redundancy as a chance for change and moved from Zürich to Sydney exchanging mountains with beaches and corporate career in the IT industry with the pleasure of networking and marketing technology.

In the meantime, corporate layoffs happen much more often now than back at that time. I faced that situation again twice since then. What does it tell me?

There is always a reason for a Pause, even without an external trigger we should press the pause button by ourselves.

Now.

Chapter 1 – The Disruption You Didn't Choose

Sometimes life presses the Pause button for us. We don't always get to choose when to start a new chapter, but we can choose what happens next from that moment.

In my case, the unexpected disruption came during what seemed like just another productive Friday. One meeting, one sentence, and suddenly the career I had built my identity around was gone. No warning. No fallback plan. Just a cup of tea hearing the sentence: "The company has decided to cancel your position."

That was the first of three layoffs that would shape the next version of myself and not because I planned it, but because I paused long enough to respond with intention.

As I detailed in my previous book, *Lead Not Manage*, I turned that layoff into a springboard for reinvention. I didn't panic; I paused. From that pause came travel, reflection, study, and eventually a move to Sydney. During that time, I discovered the power of change not as a threat, but as an invitation.

I built a framework called ROADMAP, with "Time Off" as the essential second step. That moment of stillness was not wasted time. It was strategic time, a space to break free from old routines, tune in to my values, and begin crafting new and better habits.

This book begins where so many habit journeys actually begin – with disruption. The first phase in my 4P Model is Pause: the time we stop, not because we're lazy or unfocused, but because something greater demands our attention. It could be a layoff. A breakup. A burnout. Or simply the quiet realisation that our current rhythm isn't working anymore.

"Time off is not a luxury.
It's a leadership move."

Pausing is about recalibrating direction, not stopping momentum. Only from pause can we truly see what needs to change. The resulting clarity becomes the first step to habit transformation.

The earlier mentioned book *Power of Habit* teaches us that every habit lives in a loop: cue, routine, reward. Most people try to change the routine without ever noticing the cue. But during disruption, the automatic flow is broken. That's where awareness begins.

In BJ Fogg's book *Tiny Habits* we learn that emotions create habits, not repetition alone. The emotion of disruption, such as grief or shock, becomes a fertile ground for wiring in something different within the mind – if we pause to take the time to notice.

James Clear reminds us that awareness is the first step to change. He writes in *Atomic Habits*, "Before you can effectively build new habits, you need to get a handle on your current ones. After all, if you're unaware of your habits, how can you expect to change them?"

After my first layoff, I didn't jump straight into action. I journaled. I walked. I watched patterns emerge. I started noticing not just what I was doing but why I was doing it.

This type of observation is powerful. It turns unconscious routines into conscious choices. This is where real habit change begins with awareness instead of action.

While external triggers like layoffs or major life changes often force a visible pause, some of the most powerful shifts begin quietly from the inside.

An internal trigger might be that lingering feeling of dissatisfaction after an "unsuccessful" day. Including the painful tension between how you show up publicly and how you are actually feeling within yourself.

It might come as a nagging thought like: "Is this really it?" or "Why do I keep putting this off?" or "I'm doing everything right, so why do I feel stuck?"

These internal nudges are often ignored as there is no visible disruption to explain them. They are just as valid and just as potent. They reveal a deeper truth: your habits may no longer match your evolving values.

Whether external or internal, the real trigger for habit change is awareness. Everything starts when we notice something no longer fits.

After my first layoff and the luxury of two months transition time, my wife and I went to New Zealand for three months as a trip of our lifetime. We returned to the same family in the same house where we stayed studying English after knowing each other just for half a year.

Three months without a career plan. Just with a rental car, an idea of a route, a journaling app on my iPhone, and a high need to clear my head. In the capital city of Wellington, I walked past a bookstore with a giant banner advertising the book *The Power of Habit*. I paused, thinking they had missed one letter (I write habits with a "z" all my life). This missing letter caught my attention and I stepped inside the bookshop. This was the very moment when my study of habits began.

Sometimes clarity doesn't come from a strategy session or an intended discovery. It can come from noticing a book title at the right moment in the right place.

In the first few days on this "garden leave" – as this trip with paid salary has been kindly called – I noticed something unsettling: while the world kept turning, emails were indeed answered, meetings happened without me, deals came in, and projects didn't collapse. That realisation, at first bruising, eventually became a relief.

Many people feel pressure to bounce back quickly after such a trigger. They would start polish their LinkedIn profiles and start to explain the gap before it even starts.

I did something different: I deliberately paused. My sabbatical period became the vehicle to make space for something new and not to escape from the situation.

Would I recommend everyone a trip to New Zealand? Maybe. Although that's not the point.

Pause doesn't need a passport.
It needs permission.

I began journaling because I needed to listen to myself. My Evernote app became a mirror, asking me directly what I never did before: What gives me energy? What drains me? What is automatic, and what is intentional?

Pause doesn't need to be passive; it can be productive. For me it was not the absence of progress rather the beginning of a better direction. Most of us never pause long enough to hear and listen to our inner voice on what our next move should be.

In that breathing space, I didn't just plan my next role, I started the process of designing a new rhythm. One that would be more intentional, more values-aligned, and more habit-driven.

Here you have it: an unwanted disruption can be the opener towards the required awareness before thinking at changing habits.

Chapter 1 Tasks

1. Identify your trigger point
→ Think about a recent moment of disruption in your life like external (e.g. job change, health issue, move) or internal (e.g. frustration, boredom, burnout).

→ Note down what changed and how it made you feel.

→ Be honest: was this a pause your chose or was that rather chosen for you?

2. Identify what was on autopilot
→ Name habits you became aware of that were running silently in the background.

→ List three things you routinely do without thinking.

→ Circle one that you're curious about or ready to shift.

3. Capture a new vision
→ Imagine your next chapter: what kind of person do you want to become?

→ Complete this: "I want to be someone who..."

→ Ask yourself what would that person do daily? This isn't about committing yet; just about becoming aware of a potential direction to follow.

Chapter 2 - Rewrite Your Story

When disruption hits, most people tell the story of what they have lost. Let's look at it differently: what if you could tell the story of what you found? Your unconscious mind would prefer that!

In the wake of my first layoff, I could have built a narrative around disappointment and for a while I did exactly that. It was so easy to say: "They let me go" which has a smell of "I failed". Of course I told myself: "I don't know what comes next."

Something shifted when I realised that I had a choice. I didn't control the event, but I could reframe the experience.

If I now hear someone saying, "I was made redundant", I jump into their sentence (not polite, I know) and immediately correct them: "Hey, it was just your job that was made redundant, not you as the great person you are."

What a difference!

This chapter is about mindset in a narrative way, not in the motivational sense. It's about the stories we tell ourselves after the pause and how those stories shape our identity, our energy, and our habits moving forward.

James Clear reminds us that every action is a vote for the person we want to become. But here is the challenging twist: before we cast that vote, we must believe that identity is possible and belief begins with learning from stories.

When you tell yourself "I'm not good at consistency" or "I have never been a morning person", those are not facts, rather stories which were reinforced by patterns of the past which don't need to form the future.

In my pause, I changed the story. I went from "I lost my job" to "I've been given a reset button" and from rejected to redirected.

That mental rewrite created space for a new rhythm and eventually for a new habit system.

Yes, I lost the perceived safety net of a secure role, regular salary and the illusion it would have continued forever.

Let's be honest, you don't need to pretend everything is fine. You just need to own the pen. If you're not ready to write the next chapter of your story, it is highly likely that you're unconsciously repeating the last one.

Stephen R. Covey's famous book, *The 7 Habits of Highly Effective People*, offers us timeless guidance on intentional living. The second of its foundational habits, "Begin with the end in mind", aligns perfectly with the idea of rewriting your story.

For Covey all things are created twice: first in the mind, then in action. This habit encourages readers to define a personal vision for who they want to be, long before designing how to get there.

In the context of habit formation and uncertainty of the way forward, this principle reminds us that we don't start with action – we start with identity. When we revise the internal story we tell ourselves, we begin shaping the trajectory of our behaviour.

What I highly recommend in the approach of changing habits in this identity phase is a temporary relocation to another place such as a day trip or longer to a place you like, visiting family or friends with a chance for long walks to come to yourself, or any other location that inspires you, of course not interrupted by any distraction.

The relevant insight from Covey's framework is the first habit, "Be Proactive". Rather than letting external circumstances define our future, Covey urges us to act from response-ability, our ability to choose our response.

In my own experience this is where your power lies: by taking authorship of your story after a disruption. Whether you faced a redundancy as in my example, burned out at work, or simply lost in routine, you can pause, reflect, and decide what the next chapter says about you, not what the previous one implied.

"Your habits don't just reflect your identity. They help build it – one story at a time."

This insight echoes what Dr. Maxwell Maltz discovered in his work with patients in the 1960s. In his book *Psycho-Cybernetics* he observed that people don't change their behaviour until they update their self-image which is the internal picture of who they believe they are.

Whether someone faced a life-altering experience or had a plastic surgery, the real transformation only happens when they believe something new about themselves.

Rewriting your story in a habit-building situation is not fluff, it's foundational. This is because if you still see yourself as scattered, inconsistent or just lazy, no system will stick.

Only if you start to view yourself as focused, intentional, or resilient the new habits begin to follow naturally.

In this chapter you get to choose your own self-image which is not based on what happened outside of your control but based on what is possible with you in the driver seat.

- From "I failed at this" to "I learned this is apparently not my path so what is it then?"
- From "I can't stay focused" to "I haven't found what keeps me focused yet."

This shift from judgement to curiosity is what opens the door to planning, the second P in the 4P model.

Before we build, we need to rewrite, reflect, and retell our stories. Because language shapes direction, and direction shapes behaviour.

Just ask yourself: what story have you been telling – and is it still serving you? If not, it's time to write a better one.

Chapter 2 Tasks

1. What did you lose? What did you find?

→   List three things you lost during a recent disruption, pause, or shift (e.g. certainty, routine, identity).

→   Now list three things you found or learned from that (e.g. time, resilience, perspective).

→   What surprises you most about the second list?

2. Identify a story you're ready to let go

→   Find an example story about yourselves that once served you but may no longer reflect who you are.

→   Complete this sentence: "I've been telling myself that I'm someone who...."

→   Ask yourself: "What is a better story I could tell myself now?"

3. Try on a new identity

→   Write down one identity shift you want to grow into as your next chapter.

→   Describe one small habit that another person does regularly which aligns with the future you.

→   Try it once this week. Experience and observe how it feels and plays out.

Chapter 3 – Slow Down to Speed Up

What if the key to momentum was not about doing more, but rather doing less and more deliberately?

In our world of glorified hustling, fast-tracking action and endless productivity hacks, the most counterintuitive strategy may be the most effective one: slowing down. That allows to focus and choose. It helps to clear space for direction before acceleration.

After my third layoff after just nine months in the company, I thought to do the same as I had done before which was rushing back into the market. I polished my CV, updated my cover letters, and pushed through dozens of applications. The job market was flat, the pressure was real and unlike my previous roles, this time there was no real severance to allow time to breathe. The more I pushed, the more drained I felt. I was busy but not productive. I even made it to the number two candidate in two roles.

That's when I did something radically different: I stopped. I paused the search and instead turned toward something I had already built – my book, *Connect & Act*. I leaned into consulting opportunities that aligned with my expertise around Social Selling and LinkedIn. I learned more about AI, helped two startups design their go-to-market strategies, and reconnected with what made my work meaningful in the first place.

I was still working but with calm clarity, not chaos. When the right opportunity showed up, I was not only ready for it, but I was already moving in that direction.

In *The Power of Letting Go*, John Purkiss explains that true momentum often comes only after we surrender. Not in a passive way, but in the sense of letting go of what no longer serves us such as fear, ego, and control. He writes: "The more we let go the faster we move forward."

This is not about giving up but clearing the emotional and mental clutter so that we can recognise what really matters – and act from a place of *peace* rather than *panic*. Letting go isn't a sign of weakness. It's a release that creates fresh energy for something creative and new to plant.

That's exactly what I experienced. When I stopped forcing the job hunt and let go of how things *should* unfold, I opened the door to how they *could* unfold. Consulting, writing, and learning activities flowed in when I released the grip on what wasn't working.

Cal Newport, author of *Deep Work*, puts it well: "Clarity about what matters provides clarity about what does not." That's exactly the reflective gift of slowing down. It lets you define what moves the needle and stop wasting energy on what doesn't.

This is where we transition from Pause to Plan in the 4P Model. Pausing helped you see your current habits and stories. Planning means deciding which of those habits are worth keeping and which new habits you want to design for your new life.

You don't need 17 habits. You need the right two or three, tied to the person you want to become. Planning is not about adding more tasks – instead it is about aligning behaviour with your redefined identity.

Slowing down also gives space for experimentation. You can test small changes without pressure. Try one change in your morning routine. Use a new app to track a habit. Move one habit to a different part of your day and observe the result. This kind of thoughtful iteration is how lasting change sticks.

For me it was walking and being out in the fresh air. This type of phase required a healthy body to let the brain do its job. I walked by average about seven kilometres per day. Yes, I'm blessed to live at Sydney Harbour!

From there I didn't apply for hundreds of open jobs. I applied my focus instead. From that season of clarity the next great role at my dream company came. Not because I sped up, but because I slowed down with intention.

Therefore , if you're in the messy middle between what was and what's next, please be sure that it's not a holding pattern. It's the planning ground. The space to design what comes next. Your chance for a change.

Slow down. Listen in. Realign your habits. That's how you speed up in the right direction.

Chapter 3 Tasks

1. List your loudest distractions

→ Identify three recurring distractions that pull you away from what truly matters (e.g. notifications, comparison, overcommitting).

→ For each distraction, ask: What value or need is this trying to satisfy?

→ Consider one boundary you could set to reduce its impact.

2. Define your essentials

→ List five activities, relationships, or values that energise you and align with your long-term vision.

→ Rank them in order of importance today.

→ Which one have you been neglecting the most?

3. Practise selective effort

→ Choose one thing this week to intentionally not do.

→ Replace it with a micro habit that supports one of your essentials.

→ Reflect at the end of the week: Did that change how you felt about your time, energy, or focus.

Expert Inspiration

Your story reminded me why I started the Pause Movement. It came from a time when I was tired, running on autopilot, and feeling completely disconnected even though everything looked fine from the outside. I wasn't looking for more to do. I was looking for meaning, space, and honesty.

And then something unexpected woke me up. I was looking after a gifted 9-year-old boy named Brian. Super bright. I asked him to finish his schoolwork early so I could take him out to play. He looked at me and said, "No. Because if I finish early today, my parents will just give me more work tomorrow."

That moment hit me hard. A child already learned to not finish early not because he didn't want to grow, but because he didn't feel safe. That's when it really clicked for me: this isn't just about personal wellbeing. This is about how we lead. As parents. As business owners. As humans.

When I created Pause 2025, I wanted to give leaders and business owners permission to stop and ask better questions. Not just, "How do I get more done?" but "Why am I doing all this in the first place?"

In this digital age, we have more tools than ever. But are we using them to free up time and energy to live fully? To build real-life experiences that go beyond work and tasks?

And are we creating spaces where people from all walks of life, cultures, and backgrounds feel safe to grow and thrive?

Pausing isn't weakness. It's how we check if we're heading in the right direction.

For anyone reading this chapter: Don't wait for burnout or a breakdown. Build your pause habit now. Whether it's five minutes of deep breathing, a weekly "pause walk," or a journaling check-in, let your body and mind catch up with your soul.

Let intentional pause become your practice, not just your reaction.

Rachel WingMan

Founder of Rachel WingMan Happiness Coaching (Sydney)
www.linkedin.com/in/rachelwingman

Summary

Congratulations, you made it through the first part. Now you have an idea why and how to pause on your journey to improving your habits.

Here are three key takeaways:

A sudden change breaks the rhythm of life and that break can become your breakthrough. When external circumstances force a pause, it's your chance to notice what was automatic and ask what truly matters next.

Every habit begins with a story. If the one you've been telling yourself no longer fits, it's time to update the script. Identity isn't fixed, it's flexible. Rewriting your story begins with reframing what you believe is possible.

In a world obsessed with doing more, clarity is your competitive advantage. Slowing down isn't stopping, it's focusing. By pausing the noise and letting go of pressure, you create momentum in the direction that counts.

Part 2 – Plan

"Emotions create habits. Not repetition. Not frequency. Emotions."

BJ Fogg

Design Habits That Align With Your Values

When disruption shakes your rhythm, the pause gives you a chance to notice. When your story no longer fits, you have the power to rewrite it.

Finally, when the noise settles, then you have a quiet moment to realise: "I'm ready for what comes next."

But readiness doesn't mean rushing.

In a world that rewards urgency, planning can feel slow, even unproductive. Here is the paradox: if you plan well, you will act better. You will waste less time, burn less energy, and take fewer wrong turns.

> *"Planning is not procrastination;*
> *it is preparation with purpose."*

After my own career shifts outside of the mentioned layoffs, I noticed a powerful pattern: When I didn't take enough time to plan, I fell back into reactive habits. Not bad habits necessarily, but old, familiar ones. Those which are based on a version of myself I had already outgrown.

That is the risk when we skip this phase. If we don't plan with intention, we drift back to what feels easy and not what feels aligned with our immediate future.

That's why the second part of the 4P model is **Plan**.

Not a master plan. Not a five-year vision board with well identified milestones. Rather a clear starting point with enough clarity to move forward deliberately.

Planning in this context means designing the next version of your rhythm. You will create habits that align with who you're becoming, not just who you've been.

Focus on direction, not perfection.

You will learn to set systems in motion so that the right behaviours become easier to repeat. Like a diesel engine that runs smooth and steady like clockwork once started.

One of the biggest lies in the personal growth space is the assumption that change happens with enough motivation. Well, not really. In my view change happens with enough structure – willpower alone can't provide that.

In this part of the book, you will find practical ways to:

- Connect habits to your deeper "why"
- Choose fewer priorities to execute them better
- Start small and keep it real
- Match your actions with your rewritten story

I observed that shift working was common, not just during my layoffs but especially when I intended to elevate my identity to the next level. That included moving to different countries, the next planned career step, adding my side businesses in social media and book marketing.

When I was a mentor back in Europe and in Australia, I also recognised that potential shift working for my mentees. While writing these lines I'm mentoring a young sales professional in Chicago virtually over Zoom admiring his sense of planning towards the next step in his career.

Don't mix it up: values are not goals; they are guiding principles. Your values don't change every month or year; they evolve slowly, if at all.

Values are what you stand for when the pressure is high and the options are many. If you're unsure where to begin, ask yourself when did you feel most alive or fulfilled and what behaviours from others inspire you most?

The answers to these questions reveal the themes and values. Those values will now guide the habits you choose to build.

Therefore, don't see this planning step about control, it is rather about building the confidence required to build your own habits system.

Please take what you've learned from the *Pause* step in part one and now design what comes next for you on that basis – even as there are many options and unknowns.

No need to map out your entire future. Just your next habit, your next step in your future system. Plan with purpose and align with identity. Let's get started.

Chapter 4 – Plan Like a Pro

Anyone can set goals on a positive day. Real planning is what supports you on the messy ones. And systems always win over goals.

After my first layoff back in Switzerland, it would have been easy to react: apply everywhere, scramble for anything. Rather instead, I paused, I planned. I took a different path on purpose which was a three-month journey through New Zealand to clear my mind. During that time, I made a conscious decision: I would build a new life, and that life would ideally start down under.

While I considered Auckland or Wellington, I recognised that majority of IT vendor related roles for the New Zealand market were conducted out of Australia. What a happy and convenient neighbour!

This approach of taking up the opportunity for the chance for change wasn't random. It was intentional. I wasn't reacting to a loss of the life I had, rather responding to the opportunity. Planning like a pro means designing rhythms you can sustain; not just rigid to-do lists as usual.

Did I know everything about those countries far away? Surely not. I learned a bit about living in Auckland 17 years prior to that while, studying English. Too long ago.

Planning is about choosing direction over distraction and making better decisions by default and not by force.

The first step considering change was to choose your own focus areas. However, not too many at one time.

Greg McKeown reminds us in his book *Essentialism* that success doesn't come from doing more. It rather comes from doing the right *fewer* steps and for it to be down *better*. Let me ask, which are the two to three values you stand for or the outcomes your new habits should support? Would it be about health, growth, or contribution?

Please choose your priorities with care. When your habits align with your values, the benefit is that you reduce resistance and increase motivation.

A good way to start is by asking yourself: What parts of my life do I want to feel more aligned with? Where am I overextended or drained? These questions point you to the values that need your attention and in the desired state your habits will serve these values.

Does it need an external trigger as the job loss in my case? Not really, but when it happens, the readiness is faster.

I wrote already about Charles Duhigg' book, *The Power of Habit*, which introduced the concept of keystone habits. These are foundational behaviours that spark positive chain reactions and thus create the momentum we need to achieve the desired outcome.

As a typical example think about how a daily workout habit can lead you to better nutrition experience, improved sleep, and an unexpected confidence boost.

You wouldn't achieve those three outcomes because you worked on all of that at once; they happened by executing on one well-placed habit which touched them all in one go.

When we returned from that three months journey to New Zealand which admittingly was the dream trip of our life, I was committed to keystone habits, that reflected my decision to build a new life: daily online engagement to re-connect with peers from both down under and in Europe, networking coffee chats, and posting valuable content on LinkedIn – what I have never done before. These habits didn't feel like work; they felt like an alignment – and it made me feel happy!

Setting goals in a smart way is an admirable step to foster change but it is not everything. James Clear reminds us that we don't rise to the level of our goals; we fall to the level of our systems. A great plan isn't one that looks beautiful on paper (like mine of moving down under); it's a plan that is hard to break when life gets messy.

This is where resilience comes into place. I learned early on in New Zealand with the earthquakes in Christchurch that happened between our times living there that you need to create a life with a plan B.

In terms of habits it means we need to get going even if it is tough. I observed me recording the learning in a journal. While not added enough, at least I kept going, the streak lived on. What matters here is continuity, not perfection.

When I planned my move to Sydney, it wasn't just about plane tickets and flat hunting. It was about mental preparation, emotional readiness, and habitual focus. I knew the first few months wouldn't be perfect. But I had habits that would carry me: learn the local rhythm, meet people in person, and show up on LinkedIn. I built habits that would keep me visible and connected – even when the outcome wasn't always clear.

Planning is not about mapping every minute, rather about anchoring your days in the expected meaning. A strong plan includes some level of flexibility without being rigid. I see it as a framework to work with and not as a cage.

How do you plan like a pro?

You slow down enough to clarify your values. You choose habits that connect with those values. You start small, and you make your plan resilient.

Before you practice, you plan to accept a level of the unknown. Planning sets the direction; practice builds the momentum.

Once you know where you're going, the real transformation doesn't come from the plan itself. It comes from showing up regularly.

The goal is not to have the perfect plan. Plan like a Pro is having a system that survives your real life. That way planning is not about what you do once but what you keep doing, even on a low energy day.

Chapter 4 Tasks

1. Clarify Your Focus Areas

→ Identify 1–3 focus areas that matter most to you right now (e.g. health, learning, relationships).

→ Add what is missing to achieve those focus areas.

→ Ask yourself: "If I could only move forward in these areas, would I still feel proud?"

2. Choose One Keystone Habit

→ Select one habit that would create ripple effects across your focus areas (e.g. journaling, gratitude).

→ Add more context to that keystone habit reflecting on why it is important to change now.

→ Imagine: "If I only succeeded at this one habit for 30 days, what might improve?"

3. Design a Forgiving Plan

→ Think of 1-2 obstacles that could disrupt your new habit (e.g. travel, stress, lack of motivation).

→ Create a "rescue plan" in one sentence such as: "If I miss a day, I simply pick up the next morning".

→ Design a forgiving plan for the time when you fail or things do not go in the direction you would like.

Chapter 5 - Start in Smaller Steps

Big plans feel exciting! But unfortunately, big plans often fail – not because the goal is wrong, but because the starting point is too ambitious.

After my first layoff, I made a massive shift: I moved to Australia. It was a bold decision that worked, because I had time, clarity, and motivation (and some severance money).

After my second layoff, I didn't panic. I posted instead. My habit of consistent content helped me land my next role and start in just five weeks.

But the third time was different. The job market had dried up, many tech companies recognised they hired too fast after the pandemic without sustainable demand. Sure, I applied to dozens of roles and worked my way through networking and insider connections, even made it to second place twice. But no offers. No traction. I felt burnout not from work, rather from rejection.

Therefore, I stopped pushing and paused instead. I checked at what was already working: my network, my content, and my reputation. I didn't need to chase the next job, rather I needed to build differently.

That's when consulting entered the picture. Two startup companies reached out as my book *Connect & Act* gave me the required visibility. My consistent posting built trust, the developed habits paid off.

Suddenly the miracle happened: I rejoined Hootsuite on a part-time basis for half a year. How excited to be back! To be honest: it was not the plan I had mapped out. It was a path revealed by small, consistent steps of those habits that were already in motion.

It reminded me of what BJ Fogg says in *Tiny Habits*: "Emotions create habits. Not repetition. Not frequency. Emotions." You don't need massive goals to spark change. You need emotional wins. Success momentum.

That's why I always tell everyone: if your new habit feels too small to matter, you're probably on the right track – it just didn't reveal traction yet.

Don't start with "Write a book." Have the goal in mind, maybe visualise yourself on the stage of your book launch. Then break the process into three to five parts. After that, simply start with: "Open the document."

For the more sportive type of readers: Don't start the thought process with "Run a marathon." Visualise the race, then build backwards towards a weekly running habit. Start with: "Put on your shoes."

Don't start with "Become visible online." Better picture the target audience you want to help and enhance with what makes you unique. Then begin with: "Comment on the post of someone from your ideal customer profile today."

It's really not about how much you do. It's rather about who you become by doing the required steps regularly.

When we try to overhaul everything at once, we fail. The IT support agent in your company surely doesn't change two parameters at once to fix an error, just one at a time.

When we design habits that are small, we stick with them because they're not intimidating and don't really require motivation. They just work silently in the background.

I didn't plan a consulting business in a crisis as I really love working at and contributing to SaaS companies. I just kept showing up and posted here, gave a phone call there and attended a random meeting. Playing and paying into karma. Then one day, someone said: "Hey, could we talk about a short-term project?"

That's how small habits work to get wheels in motion. They don't just help you feel better like providing instant gratification. They create opportunities.

Fogg's *Tiny Habits* method teaches us to pair some new behaviours with existing routines so that the new habit doesn't stand just by itself but finds an already established partner. He wrote: "After I pour my morning coffee, I will..." This technique is called habit stacking. It's deceptively simple and highly effective.

Too many people set themselves a day for a change like a New Year Resolution but totally miss to add what they want to change towards an already established routine that they have no problem in conducting. That little connection can be put into practice easier than something totally new.

Do you want to become someone who reflects? Stack a journaling habit after brushing your teeth. Want to stretch more? Do it after you close your computer for the day.

The point is not the size of the action; it's the consistency of the cue. That's how identity shifts begin. If you still feel unsure, please combine it with a reward you usually give yourself anyway and add the new habit just before that.

Every time I posted on LinkedIn, I was reinforcing an identity: I am someone who shows up. And believe me, as a born introvert that was not an easy task for too many years.

Only rarely a post went viral (which means hitting about three times my followers). But every post built trust. After a couple of weeks people noticed. And after some months, it built something more into the habit-built opportunities.

This is how you start like a pro. Do not go too big. Instead, be consistent. Please let go of the pressure of doing more, better perform smaller steps than you think.

And that's where the real growth happens – not in the sprint itself, but in the rhythm and routine. You surely know the analogy "sprint vs. marathon" which we need to modify a bit – we need to sprint to get started (like starting an old diesel engine) and then add the rhythmic marathon element to it.

Here we have it: you don't need more motivation; you need a well-chosen set of micro-moves.

Start today. Start tiny. Start now.

Chapter 5 Tasks

1. Define your meaningful target
→ What's a personal goal you want to work towards?

→ Break it into 3–5 smaller components or milestones.

→ Circle the smallest starting point for you this week.

2. Stack your habit to something you already do
→ Use the *Tiny Habits* formula: "After I [existing habit], I will [new habit]."

→ Choose something you already do daily (e.g. grab your coffee, check email).

→ Match it with a micro-habit (e.g. write one sentence in your journal, open a document, stretch for one minute) and test it for three days.

3. Redefine success as showing up
→ Write down a habit you want to start.

→ Ask yourself: "What's the tiniest version I could commit to, even on my worst day?"

→ Try it today and celebrate that accordingly.

Chapter 6 – Repeatable Rhythms

Your big plans live in your head. Real change lives in your calendar.

I was born in the city of Bremen in Germany and later shaped by Swiss precision when I emigrated to Zurich. For me the word discipline has a deep meaning which my move to Australia didn't remove from me.

However, even with a natural leaning towards a positive structure, I had to learn one key lesson: motivation may get you started, but rhythm keeps you going.

When I reflect on the habits that changed my business life – such as my weekly #socialsellingmonday LinkedIn posts, my monthly webinars, the curious coffee chats – none of them happened by accident. I built them into my week; they became rhythm.

When videographer Jason Knight inspired me to write a post series and executive coach Duncan Fish supported me at a meeting at a BNI FACE chapter in November 2018, I blocked the time and started writing. Keeping the promise of the intended six weeks, I just added it into the calendar.

While writing these lines, I visited that particular BNI chapter six years later and thanked them that this approach changed my career for the better. Even in a double sense as my visa consultant with the initial advice on how to move to Australia became a member of the same BNI chapter.

Greg McKeown added this wisdom in his remarkable book *Essentialism*: "If you don't prioritize your life, someone else will." It's not just that, I would add if you don't design your default week, the chaos of others will design it for you. In other words, be in control of your own time.

Back in the days I gave multiple Microsoft Outlook Lunch & Learn trainings – not to train the functions but rather to elaborate on how it can eliminate useless elements to keep the calendar clean without overplanning.

Now you reached the point in the book where we stop planning in theory and start integrating our desired habits into reality.

The intended rhythm enables you to place anchors in your day instead of controlling every hour. These are repeatable cues and containers for the things that matter.

Let me show you some examples that worked for me well over the years:

Time blocking: If I want something to happen, I give it a place in my calendar. Just like you wouldn't miss a doctor's appointment, I don't miss my weekly LinkedIn post or an important strategy session. What's not booked is at risk.

Energy mapping: I observed when I do my best deep work (I'm an early morning bird), when I should ideally take meetings (early afternoons, not right after lunch), and when to reflect or reset (late afternoons). Aligning habit types to energy zones matters, and this is different for everyone.

Habit bundling: I'm a fan of pairing a small routine with something already in place. After my first coffee in a café outside (deliberately not owning a coffee machine), I open my post drafts. After wrapping a Zoom call, I send one thoughtful message to the participants from a selection of templates. Small rituals create momentum.

Weekly reset: Every Sunday evening I ask myself: what's working, what's slipping, what needs to shift? It's maybe just ten minutes that keeps my rhythm intentional – and allows me to sleep well as these thoughts are already covered.

Discipline without rhythm leads to burnout. Rhythm without intention leads to drift. Yet what about discipline *with* rhythm? That's where sustainable growth happens!

Don't forget: your calendar is not a prison, rather a permission slip to design the life you actually want to create! Choose your repeatable elements and habits wisely.

I already mentioned my regular LinkedIn series which started with intention and then became an identity. Interesting that most professionals I meet don't struggle with *ideas* as they believe, instead they struggle with *systems*.

Many of them told me: "I want to post more" or "How can I be more active on LinkedIn?" When they get to the app or on their browser then the desired action simply freezes.

No plan, no prompts, no templates. Without a simple process in place, the long-awaited habit slips. The desired rhythm never begins.

When I wanted to play on the piano without sheet music in front of me I actually couldn't do that despite I had the systems in place as a young boy after eight years of practice.

It reminds me of fitness. My brother Holger is a regular jogger. Doesn't matter if it is an early morning, if it rains or shines, off he goes as long as his workplace allows. Despite it's not really my thing (except Nordic Walking), I respect his approach as I see what it takes: not motivation, but preparation. Shoes at the door? Route planned? Gear ready? Go!

The same goes for content habits. If you want to become a regular contributor, start by reducing friction. In my LinkedIn course and my book, *Connect & Act*, I provided templates with content ideas and suggestions how to invite with a personalised message.

You will find your own rhythm to use templates, create a content ad-hoc or from a batch process, or repurpose your best material in a new context. Just find your rhythm.

Here's the trick: even if you're consistent in one area of your life such as like running, journaling, or meal preparation, you can borrow that structure and apply it to a new habit. You already know how rhythm feels. Now bring it where you want to change.

Put your values on the calendar. Make your habits visible. Give them a rhythm that reflects your real life. Momentum is earned in the rhythm of well-designed days and not built in a single breakthrough action.

Chapter 6 Tasks

1. Map your natural rhythm
→ Identify your peak energy times during the day (e.g. morning focus, afternoon dip).

→ What types of habits could you place in each zone?

→ Mark one small habit for each: high, medium, and low energy periods.

2. Create a weekly rhythm anchor
→ Choose one habit or ritual you commit to repeat weekly (e.g. reflection, content, walk).

→ Block a recurring day and time in your calendar.

→ What needs to shift to protect this time?

3. Transfer rhythm from one area to another
→ Think of an area where you already have a good discipline (e.g. fitness, journaling).

→ What systems, reminders, or prep steps make it work?

→ Apply that rhythm to a new habit you want to build. What could that look like?

Expert Inspiration

In May 2020, I stopped drinking alcohol overnight. Not because I had a problem with alcohol, but because I finally saw all the problems that alcohol was creating in my life.

I recognised the pattern: drinking was my go-to coping mechanism and self-care method, yet it was triggering anxiety, tiredness, and disconnection from the person I wanted to be: inspiring, healthy, and happy! The day I realised that this was one habit I could control, everything changed. I saw how removing one unconscious behaviour could create a ripple effect of clarity, energy, and wellbeing. That's the power of self-awareness, and I did it.

As I often tell my clients: stick to the plan, not the mood. A "happy life" isn't a destination, rather a string of happy moments. We miss them when we're stuck on autopilot, without a plan, and waiting for everything to align for happiness.

Humans have around 60,000 thoughts per day. But what is truly concerning is that 75% of these thoughts are negative, and 95% are the same, day after day. Which means that until we boost our self-awareness and take control of our thoughts, our life will also feel out of control.

Planning brings your life back into your hands. It's how you hop off autopilot: you bring your habits to your consciousness, and instead you start creating rituals that support how you want to feel and live.

Start small: a morning ritual, a transition routine, a new coping mechanism, or a five-minute check-in before bed.

As this book *Happy Habits* reminds us, planning aligns your energy with what matters most.

Want to feel happier? Hop off autopilot. Plan for joy. Plan for connection. Plan for health. Then savour those moments. That's where happiness lives.

Sophie Anderson

Wellness Coach for Thriving Workplace at Cairns Coaching (Cairns)

www.linkedin.com/in/sophanderson

Summary

Well done, you also completed the second part. Now you know how to plan your approach towards working on your habits.

Here are three key takeaways:

Transform disruption into direction by designing sustainable systems, not fragile goals. Align habits with values and keystone actions to create momentum, even when life gets messy or complicated.

Ambition fails without traction. Build identity through micro-moves. Your smallest consistent step – paired with emotion and timing – creates real change. Start tiny, show up daily, and let trust build opportunity.

Discipline becomes sustainable when structured into rhythm. Time blocking, habit bundling, and energy mapping turn ideas into consistent actions inside your own calendar. Rhythm beats motivation every time.

Part 3 - Practice

"You do not rise to the level of your goals.
You fall to the level of your systems."

James Clear

Repeat and Refine Over Time

You've paused. You've planned. Now comes the part that feels both simple and hard: Practice.

This is where ideas become action, where small steps meet real life and where change stops being something you think about and becomes something you live through.

But here's the truth: most people get stuck right here. They overthink the start, wait for a better time, and expect consistency to come from motivation and yet in reality, it comes from rhythm and reputation.

I've watched people map out brilliant goals, only to fall short when routines break (me included).

And I've seen others with humble habits outperforming everyone around them, simply because they kept showing up again and again.

This part of the book is about showing up and building the rhythm that works for you.

You don't need to be perfect, don't even need a 5.00 am routine as some gurus show on Instagram.

What you need is a structure that helps you stay in the game, especially when life gets tough.

Routines are underrated because they're not glamorous. They don't make headlines and they don't spike dopamine. Still, if you really think about it: they are the backbone of every transformation you admire.

When someone creates great work, builds a thriving business, or becomes a pillar in their community – it's rarely a result of overnight magic. It's the outcome of repeatable, deliberate rhythms and planning that compound over time.

In this section, we'll explore how to:

- Build systems instead of relying on willpower
- Use energy wisely to avoid burnout
- Anchor your actions to existing cues in your day
- Recover and reset when life gets in the way
- And above all, keep going

In German we often say: "Übung macht den Meister." Literally it means "Practice creates the master" which for me sounds better than the regular translation "Practice makes perfect" as we will never be perfect.

But there's more about it: those who master something aren't always the most talented, they're the ones who just don't stop putting their reps in.

Whether it's weekly writing, consistent job applications, regular check-ins with clients and partners, or as in my case playing the piano again after decades: what matters most is intentional repetition.

You'll notice that rhythm is different from routine. Rhythm allows you to be flexible and respond. It breathes within you and shifts your mood which may accumulate.

Remember when you get into a flow with your fitness, meditation, or writing practice? Then you know this feeling; I just experienced this through the completion of this book in one long writing session. You miss repeating activities when you skip them. That's the power of rhythm.

Of course, real life brings interruptions. Health setbacks, job stress, family needs; it's unrealistic to expect a flawless streak. So instead of aiming for streaks, we aim for recovery. This section will show you how to reset without guilt and start again without shame.

Part 3 of *Happy Habits* is where your efforts begin to stick. You may already have one or two rhythms that work for you. The next step is to apply that same thinking to the habits you want to build now.

If you go jogging twice a week, you already understand discipline. If you cook dinner every night for your family, you already know structure.

Now we need to transfer that inner capacity you already know to the habits that matter most today. You know that works for little things so why not adopting it for larger ones?

At this part of the journey, you work on reinforcing your identity through repetition. Eventually, you will see over time that your actions don't *reflect* your values, they *become* them.

Time to move from practice to progress, one rhythm at a time. Let's get to work. Now!

Chapter 7 – Build Without Burnout

Some people break their developed habits because of a burnout. Others break because their habits caused it.

Let's be clear: building better habits in our lives is more about designing followed by a smarter process rather than just pushing harder. If your plan demands perfection, you're not building a real system, rather setting a trap.

After my third layoff just nine months from the previous one, I nearly fell into that trap. I applied to dozens of roles, often second place. My days were filled with rejections. I wasn't burned out from overwork; I was burned out from trying to stay hopeful without traction or leads.

I slowed down because I needed to preserve my energy. This was not about giving up! I picked up consulting work instead and supported two startups. I rejoined Hootsuite part-time as my headcount didn't exist. What looked like a survival role was the start of something sustainable.

I didn't build a habit that drained me or rejected the idea that sending CVs was a good habit to have. I built one that fits for me, one that protected me while I rebuilt.

This is where the idea of the minimum viable habit comes in which sounds a bit like the well-known MVP – the minimum viable product. Here it is the smallest version of a habit that still casts a vote for the person you want to become.

BJ Fogg famously said: "Floss one tooth." This is what gets you started. When the barrier is tiny, the odds of action go up and sometimes, that's all you need.

In his book *Essentialism*, Greg McKeown found another way to express that and wrote: "Do less, but better." You need a rhythm you can live with especially on your worst day, not a high-intensity routine.

That's why I encourage people to start with what I call energy-aware habits. When the energy is low, you just can't execute your regular habits. Getting back to the level you had seems impossible.

Start by mapping your typical week. When do you feel fresh? When do you feel flat? Assign your high-energy habits (like deep work or physical training) to your peak times. Schedule gentle habits (like journaling or stretching) for the low-energy windows.

This has often been a discussion in job interviews when I declared what type of tasks I would perform at which time of the day to balance high demanding tasks from more routine ones based on habits, not just because I have to do them.

You don't need to master perfect time management; you better master your energy management which increases your motivation and in turn you will be more productive.

Watch your signals such as fatigue, frustration, or feeling off. Your personal system tells you something is misaligned. Don't ignore those messages; instead adjust accordingly.

Too many people think habits are only working if they're growing. Although a habit that sustains you, even quietly, is a habit worth celebrating.

On my harder days, I still opened my MacBook and wrote a post. Sometimes it wasn't great. Sometimes it didn't get noticed but I showed up and that's what kept the rhythm alive and protected momentum.

The truth is: any habit worth having needs to survive your real life. In real life there will be setbacks, stress, and slumps.

The question is: will your habits collapse under pressure, or flex to carry you through? Better design flexible habits that support you and feel like an ally, not a threat.

Burnout isn't always loud. Sometimes it arrives quietly through chronic tension, emotional flatness, or the growing resistance to do what once felt easy. That's why your habits must include recovery, not just progress. Think of rest as an essential ritual, not a reward.

The best systems value sustainability over productivity and honour your limits while holding space for your growth. A positive habit holds you together on your worst days instead of only cheering at your best. When you design your systems with care, your habits become a shelter and a structure, not a stressor. That's real resilience.

Don't break yourself for performing a habit when you can't. Better build a habit that protects you.

Chapter 7 Tasks

1. Define your minimum viable habit

→ Choose a habit you would like to maintain even on tough days.

→ What is the smallest version of that habit?

→ Write it out and commit to it for five days this week, even if only for 30 seconds.

2. Map Your Energy-Aware Week

→ Divide your typical day into these three zones: high, medium, and low energy.

→ Assign one habit to each zone (e.g. deep work in high, walking in medium, journaling in low).

→ Sketch your rhythm as a calendar or timeline.

3. Recognise and Respond to Signals

→ Think about at a time when you felt depleted. What signs showed up (e.g. tension, procrastination, mood)?

→ Write down three personal burnout flags.

→ For each flag, write one way you could adjust or simplify your habit in response.

Chapter 8 – Recover Like a Pro

There is a myth in the world of habits that once you fall off track, you're back at zero. As if every skipped workout or missed journal entry wipes the slate clean.

The truth is: habits go on quietly, they don't disappear. Recovery is part of the rhythm as a re-entry, not a reset.

I know this because of something that used to be part of me: the piano. I played for eight years as a young boy. Sheet music, practice routines, recitals, even certificates at the Conservatorium of Music. Then I stopped. Life moved on, and the keys went silent.

While writing this book, I sat down at a piano again, first without sheet music, just using my muscle memory. This way I realised something important: the notes were rusty, but the identity remained. I wasn't really starting from scratch, rather from a pause. And as soon as I got fresh sheet music and a purpose of what to play, the joy continued!

That's how habit recovery works. You don't completely erase what you've built. You return to it, slowly and gently. It feels like warming up an old melody – or like regaining the muscle back after years of absence from the gym.

Professionals recover differently and typically don't guilt themselves for slipping. They just resume without drama and without shame. This is what makes them consistent by using resilience, not striving perfection.

What is the biggest mistake I see? People trying to pick up right where they left off using the same intensity and frequency. Re-entry isn't a sprint, rather a soft launch some levels lower than before.

When I returned to the piano, I didn't begin straight away with playing Beethoven. I began with basic scales as in Mozart's simple etudes. The win wasn't playing perfectly but to sit down at the keys and find the passion again.

Habits work the same way. If you stopped writing, post a sentence. If you missed your walk, go around the block. If you fell behind in learning, read one page.

This is where your systems matter including templates, routines, and cues. They help you get back into rhythm without friction. The more you've prepped, the easier it is to return.

Professionals don't just build habits; instead they build welcoming pathways back to their habits. Those pathways are like a reminder or reset button built in.

Ask yourself: What would make it easier to return if I slipped? A checklist? A note from my past self? A friend I text when I need to resume? Your habit is just waiting to be restarted, it's not broken!

Some of the best things I've built came after a pause. When I came back, I had a new perspective, and that is what some of our habits are missing: the context about applying the new habits will eventually matter.

Recover like a pro, start smaller or start slower, but at least start again. It is important to ensure that you don't lose your identity just because you missed a week. If anything, how you return to a habit strengthens who you are.

Once I read this sentence: "Perfectionism breaks more habits than failure ever did."

The goal here is to return faster to your initially built habit – but with grace, clarity, and your hands on the keys again. Even now, when I sit at the piano, I play to reconnect, not to impress.

Maybe music is not your topic? Then think of physical training: after time off, a smart coach doesn't push you to max weights or intense sessions on day one. Instead, they focus on form, breath, and short reps. Why? Because re-entry is about pacing, not punishment. Our muscles remember without completely forgetting, but they also need care.

The same goes for mental and emotional habits. You might need lighter reps, shorter sessions, or even a warm-up period. That doesn't mean you're weak, it's wise to return in a slower way. Fitness experts call this a "deload phase" which is a period of reduced volume to rebuild strength.

We can borrow that idea: when life gets heavy, reduce the load, not the habit. Protect the habit's core, even if you can't do the full version.

Recovery is not the opposite of discipline. It is part of it and brings you back to what really matters.

Chapter 8 Tasks

1. Identify a paused habit

→ Think of a habit you once had but stopped (e.g. journaling, walking, posting).

→ Write down what that habit gave you at its best.

→ Ask yourself: What is a good small way you could restart it this week?

2. Create a re-entry ritual

→ Design a simple ritual to welcome yourself back into a habit (e.g. a playlist, use favourite mug, setup a 5-min reset routine).

→ Write it out as a checklist or sentence.

→ Use it next time you feel off track.

3. Reframe the story

→ Complete this sentence: "I used to think missing a habit meant I failed. Now I know it means..."

→ Replace judgment with curiosity.

→ Write one compassionate phrase you'll use next time you slip.

Chapter 9 – When Habits Get Messy

There's a moment in every habit journey when the system you've built starts to wobble: Life interrupts, plans shift and focus fades. The rhythm you've established so hard feels off-beat. This is the chapter for those moments.

It's easy to maintain a habit when everything is going well, when motivation is high, sleep is solid, and the calendar is under control. Habits are not just built and applied in ideal conditions. They're strengthened in messy chaotic ones.

The problem is that most people treat inconsistency as failure. They miss one day and assume they've undone all their progress. Skipping once is not the issue. The issue is the story you tell yourself after skipping.

This chapter is about making your habits stick through flexibility. Resilient systems recover; fragile systems crack.

Here's the reality: there will be travel, illness, deadlines, or setbacks. Instead of planning your habits that work only in perfect scenarios, build ones that adapt.

A small example: let's assume your regular routine is to journal for ten minutes each morning. On this particular day you overslept, your inbox exploded and there's no time. What if you wrote just one sentence instead?

This is what James Clear calls "standardizing before you optimize." You don't need to do it well; you just need to do it. Protect the identity, even if the output is small.

I've seen this with many professionals. The ones who keep growing are the ones who return faster after going through a disruption.

Chapter 6 covered consistency from the psychological angle. Here we look at it situationally: what do you do when your ideal routine is impossible? You adapt. You scale it down. You shift the form but keep the function.

Let's say you usually go to the gym for an hour. This week you're travelling. Could you do 15 push-ups in your hotel room? Could you stretch while watching the news? Replacing your habit with something similar prevents you from restarting after your return to the usual rhythm.

Progress isn't erased by a single deviation. Perfectionism often leads to abandoning the habit altogether, a total trap (coming from Switzerland we love our perfectionism).

The key insight: Don't judge the habit by the outcome. Judge it by the ease of return to the regular rhythm. Every system needs to tolerate disruption which includes your personal routines. Build in margins and buffer. Have a Plan B that still reinforces your identity.

I always admired smokers for having that extra ten minutes to smoke before a customer meeting which they could easily eliminate if they would arrive later than expected. I didn't build that buffer in my travel plans as I didn't have a similar ritual in place. I still remember sitting in the office of Philip Morris as the only non-smoker in the room.

One client of mine used to meditate every morning for 15 minutes. When his newborn arrived, mornings became chaos. Instead of quitting, he shifted to three deep breaths while the coffee brewed. While this was not the same habit it still pointed to the same identity in a mindful way. It was an adjustment yet still a practice that was adopted.

This a quote I love: "The best swimmers are not the ones who never swallow water. They're the ones who recover their rhythm the quickest."

When GoTo laid me off after just nine months in the company, I didn't panic – I posted instead. Not because I had a polished plan, but because I had a practiced habit.

The job market was different than the year before as many companies reduced their teams as a response to demand changes in a post-covid world.

Just two weeks earlier, I had launched my Social Selling book *Connect & Act*, built entirely from weekly LinkedIn posts. The habits of writing, showing up, and staying visible didn't just help me write the book; they now helped me land consulting work that paid 30 times more than my royalties.

What made the difference? I didn't wait to feel ready. I kept the rhythm. And when the storm hit, my habit became my anchor.

When habits get messy, don't strive to be perfect. Instead strive to return and to adapt. That's how you make your habits stick and improve.

Chapter 9 Tasks

1. Notice the noise

→ Reflect on when life disrupted your routine.

→ What kind of internal dialogue showed up? (e.g. guilt, frustration, excuses)

→ Write down two or three common thoughts that surface when habits slip.

2. Create a Gentle Restart Plan

→ Identify a habit you've dropped recently (or one you fear dropping).

→ Design a soft re-entry version of that which is smaller, easier, and with lower friction.

→ What would make it welcoming to return to? (e.g. playlist, reminder, visual cue)

3. Build a messy day version

→ Choose one habit you're currently working on.

→ Now write a "messy day" variation of that which you could still do if tired, stressed, overcommitted or distracted.

→ Practice this fallback version once this week.

Expert Inspiration

When founders come to me, they're not usually short on vision, they're overwhelmed by friction. Their teams stall. Their projects stall. They stall.

Not because they don't know what to do, but because they haven't built the system to keep doing it.

That's why I always return to one idea: habits aren't goals, they're systems. They're not motivation, they're rhythm. In operations, we don't win with heroics. We win with consistency.

This applies just as much in personal life. I start everyday with push-ups, and I've been doing it almost every day for over 25 years. It wakes me up with a positive mindset early in the day. Has there been lapses in this rhythm? Yes, and I just ease back into doing it, by committing to just doing a few push-ups, and in no time at all, I'm back where I was.

I've built my week like a playlist, tasks match my energy, and that flow keeps me in the game even when life throws curveballs.

The trick isn't doing everything. It's making the important things easier to repeat. Just like in business: if a task is important, you don't leave it to chance, you document it, assign it, and build a habit around it.

On rough days, I don't aim for high performance. I aim to protect momentum. A few sentences in a post. A 15-

minute review instead of a full strategy session, these are "minimum viable habits", still pointing at the identity I'm trying to reinforce.

Your habits shouldn't break when life does. They should flex. Rigid routines collapse under pressure. But well-built rhythms? They bend, they breathe, and they bring you back.

If your habits feel fragile, don't throw them out. Build a softer version. Practice the return. That's where real resilience lives.

Lloyd Thompson

Founder of VirtualDOO, author of "9 Ways to Leave Your Day to Day Operations" (Sydney)

www.linkedin.com/in/lloydt

Summary

Congratulations, you made it through the third part. Now you have a good understanding on the practice side towards habits with resilience that stand difficult times.

Here are three key takeaways:

Rhythm builds resilience. Once you've paused and planned, the next step is presence instead of perfection. This is where habits take shape through repetition, not by using pressure.

Real life rarely runs smoothly. That's why your habits need to bend, not break. By choosing systems over will-power and designing habits that flex with your energy, you build routines that hold up even when the day doesn't.

Recovery is an important part of the cycle, not failure. When habits go quiet, they're not completely gone. Re-entry becomes easier when you lower the bar, honour your capacity, and return with grace.

Part 4 – Partner

"The right people will help you achieve the right things."

Greg McKeown

Create Accountability and Shared Momentum

Welcome to the fourth and final part of this book where we explore a powerful truth: the best habits are rarely built alone by individuals.

Once you've paused, planned, and practiced your way into new rhythms, the question becomes: how do you keep going, especially when motivation fades and life becomes busy or unpredictable?

The answer lies in partnership; not only in the business sense as in my profession. With partnership I mean the deeper, human sense of alignment, encouragement, and a shared direction.

In the book *Essentialism*, the British American author Greg McKeown urges us to do less, but better. His lens isn't focused on hustle or doing more, but on the intentional elimination of what doesn't matter. By focusing only on the essential, we gain clarity and strength.

One particularly memorable chapter in his book explores the power of buffers. That means systems and people who help us navigate life's friction. When applied to habits, those buffers are often others – habit buddies.

You achieve that with well-chosen partners to become like a family routine with the benefit of accountability groups. These relationships help us internalise discipline.

Greg McKeown reminds us: "When we have strong routines and strong relationships, we're far more resilient." I couldn't agree more living and breathing partnerships.

Whether it's as simple as sending a Monday check-in or as significant as building a shared creative practice, your chances of success multiply when someone else is invested in your effort, not just in your outcome.

In *Happy Habits*, this final part is called Partner because success doesn't need to feel solitary.

By writing weekly content using the same topic and hashtag for years, I was connecting with a community, not just building a habit. The consistency built trust, and the trust led to collaboration.

When I hosted my networking events with workshop style I made sure to have a momentum that the participants created something together. A conclusion coming from a group exercise turning into an aha moment is much better than a slide of theoretical wisdom noted by others.

When I reflect on moments of struggle, in my case through layoffs, transitions, or creative blocks, what helped me through was not willpower as many gurus wanted me to believe.

Instead it was talking to people, especially those who nudged me, checked in, or simply reminded me I wasn't alone. These were the moments when I have been grateful that I build my strong network before I needed it.

Partnership for me is more about a shared motion than an outsourcing effort of split actions. It feels like a boat you row together or a rhythm built side by side.

That is the essence of this section: when your habits are shared, they gain power. Shared routines build resilience, shared intentions create alignment, and shared effort creates a momentum that lasts longer than discipline ever could.

As we enter the final three chapters in this book, ask yourself not just "What habits will I keep?" but also "Who will I build them with?"

In every great story, transformation doesn't happen in isolation. As in Mozart's opera *The Magic Flute*, the hero's journey is marked by various tests, unexpected allies, and eventual transcendence. Tamino can't succeed alone; he grows through challenge, supported by friendship, love, and shared purpose.

His path mirrors our own: initial resistance, trials that stretch us, and relationships that strengthen us. True habits shape character and sustain impact, especially when they emerge from connection.

As your journey continues, remember that even the hero needs a companion. Your rhythm becomes so much richer when others walk or play alongside you.

In the end, lasting change is more about who you bring with you instead of who you become by yourself.

Now and forever.

Chapter 10 – Don't go Alone

Habits are personal but they don't have to be lonely. One of the most powerful truths I've learned on this journey is well known: we go further when we go together.

That's why the best habits aren't hidden but shared. For strength not for show. Reminds me at the Swedish proverb:

> *"Shared joy is a double joy;*
> *shared sorrow is half a sorrow."*

Accountability is underrated and it gets a bad reputation. People hear the word and imagine ongoing pressure, a negative feeling of guilt, or someone breathing down their neck.

Real accountability is about being seen cheering on the journey. It's about having someone who cares enough to ask, "How is it going?"

After publishing dozens of book reviews and interviews with fellow published authors, I noticed something: I was more consistent when others were involved. A co-guest, a reader waiting, or a shared deadline. Those subtle forms of visibility turned intention into succeeded follow-through.

I've also seen this through habit check-ins with peers. Sometimes, it's just a weekly text like: "Did you do your Tuesday post?" Sure, I could have checked it by myself but asking is more powerful to show that we indeed care.

A good tip is a shared folder with progress updates. There is no pressure and requirement to do that; it feels as a positive reminder that someone is in your corner.

Let's break it down. I found three simple types of gentle accountability:

1. Visibility: When your habit is shared publicly, even passively. Like a weekly newsletter, a visible log, or a recurring hashtag. You don't need to ask for feedback but you're showing up.

2. Shared Practice: You're not performing alone. You co-work, co-write, and co-walk. You have a rhythm that syncs with someone else. And that rhythm creates motivation.

3. Check-in Support: Someone who asks about your progress to care, not to judge. This can be a coach, a friend, a partner, or even a community Slack channel.

Think of this as your personal support stack. Not everything has to be public, not everyone needs to know that. But having even *one* person aware of your intention changes how you show up.

When I teach group programs, I encourage participants to declare just one goal and then post their update in the group once a week. No likes needed. The act of sharing is what matters.

In my corporate roles I mentored many younger sales professionals. I often took this as a chance to practice what I call reverse mentoring. That makes me accountable as well and it feels much more participate for my mentee.

You can build your own stack like this:

- A habit buddy who checks in every Monday
- A shared tracker (like Notion or Google Sheets) to log wins and record the learning
- A calendar block labelled with your goal
- A ritual cue (like a coffee + journal) that sets the rhythm
- A declared reward (e.g. watching your Netflix show or socialising with a friend after a task is completed)

Here's the key: Let it feel light. Accountability that drains you isn't working. Support should feel like encouragement, not expectation. When someone cheers you on as a companion and not a micro manager then you don't feel watched. You rather feel accompanied and supported.

This approach becomes even better when you participate in their challenges as well – that is the Law of Reciprocity from Robert Cialdini's book, *Influence: The Psychology of Persuasion*, in action.

Don't go alone. Your habits deserve company. Because when we share the rhythm, we double the resilience.

Chapter 10 Tasks

1. Choose Your Habit Buddy

→   Think of someone who could support your goal (a friend, peer, or colleague).

→   Ask: "Would you be open to a weekly check-in?"

→   Set a simple rhythm with them: a Monday message, a Friday review, or a shared log.

2. Pick a Public Signal

→   Choose one habit you're willing to make visible.

→   Use a tracker, hashtag, or recurring update (e.g. "Thursday Thoughts" posts).

→   Write out when and how you'll share it this week.

3. Design Your Support Stack

→   List tools or people that could help you staying more consistent.

→   Try various versions like a Notion page, a habit group, a progress sticker on your calendar.

→   Label them with Visibility / Shared Practice / Check-In.

Chapter 11 – Habits to Strengthen Relationships

Not every habit is about you. Some of the most powerful ones are about *them*.

We often think of habits as a personal improvement tool such as morning routines, fitness streaks, journaling rituals. In my experience, the habits that truly shape our lives are the ones that strengthen our relationships.

Networking, at its best, is the act of showing up again and again with presence, attention, and care. Those who collect business cards by the quantity misunderstand connection as collection.

I learned this over hundreds of coffee chats, post-event follow-ups, and quiet check-ins. Not because I was always trying to get something out for me. I understood this simple truth: relationships compound, just like habits.

When someone tells me they struggle with networking, I ask them: "What's your rhythm?" If theirs is based only on events or occasional bursts, no wonder it feels inconsistent.

When they build simple rituals like sending a message the day after an event, tagging a person in a relevant article, or checking in one month after a connection they are just creating something deeper: trust.

This is what I call relationship rituals. Here are a few of them I return to quite often:

- The gratitude loop: Saying thanks with context such as "Thanks again for the intro to Alex. We had a great call."

- Thinking of you: Sending a podcast, article, or opportunity because it will be valuable for them, without expectation.

- Regular touches: A quick check-in with someone you just met or reconnected with. Just to tell them, "Still thinking of our chat."

These aren't marketing tactics. They're micro-habits of connection and communication and they neither take much time nor do they need perfect templates, just intention and follow through.

My weekly habit of posting with #socialsellingmonday has created more than visibility. It created the perception of continuity, backed by the fact that I didn't miss a week since 2018. People remember consistency. When you apply that to your relationships, people begin to rely on your presence.

Even a simple comment or a kind mention can keep the relationship warm. Over time, these touches build something far stronger than a CRM ever could: human memory.

You can try this: each week, choose a person you haven't spoken to in a while and send them a meaningful message. Not a pitch. Not a request. Just a human hello. This is how you turn an occasional effort into a habit.

If you want to build stronger relationships, build rituals like this that make you easier to remember for them. Just make sure to act with their interest in mind as nothing feels worse than recognising a hidden agenda.

When people feel seen, they respond. And when they trust you'll show up more than once, then you stop being a connection. You become a partner. Remember: partnership is the principle on which 75% of the world trade is based.

Relationship habits don't have to be random. Like your physical environment which shapes your personal habits, your social environment shapes how you show up for others.

I keep gentle cues in place: a recurring calendar block for coffee catch ups (and a Google Sheet to track them including notes and photos), a dedicated "connections" column in my weekly journal, and reminders to follow up after events.

These aren't suitable rhythm builders which you could also understand as productivity hacks. When your system supports your social intention, you don't have to rely on memory or motivation.

Habits don't just help you do more or achieve more. They help you build better relationships. And when that is heartfelt and comes as a surprise it makes the other person feel happy.

Here we have it: *Happy Habits* is not just the title of this book. Developing good habits with a partnership mindset can result in mutual happiness.

Chapter 11 Tasks

1. Create Your Relationship Ritual
→ Choose a recurring relationship habit you'd like to build (e.g. check-in, gratitude message, follow-up).

→ Decide when and how to do it (e.g. "Every Friday at 3pm, send one message").

→ Add it to your calendar or habit tracker.

2. Practice the Gratitude Loop
→ Identify someone you appreciate but haven't followed up with recently.

→ Send a message by expressing thanks and mentioning what stuck with you.

→ Reflect on how it felt to write and send it.

3. Keep One Connection Warm
→ Pick a contact you haven't spoken to in 1–3 months.

→ Send a "saw this and thought of you" note, share a quick update, or just say hello.

→ Repeat this weekly for one month.

Chapter 12 - Create a Shared Journey

By now, you've paused, planned, and practiced your way toward better habits. You've explored ways how to stay consistent and how to recover. This final step is where it all comes together when your habits stop being a solo act and become part of a shared rhythm.

When I introduce myself at partner events, people quickly notice I'm not a native English speaker. So I offer a little linguistic insight: in German, the word for partnership is *Partnerschaft*. Interestingly, the word *Partner* is the same, but *schafft* means "he/she works".

There's a common saying among many German Partner Managers: "Partnership is when the partner works." To be honest, I've never liked that phrase.

To me, real partnership isn't about someone else doing the work; I prefer the analogy of being in the same boat. Built into the English word partner*ship*, it is like a vessel you navigate together through calm and current, in wind and wave.

I used this analogy in an internal online course I created when I worked at Hootsuite which I called *Partnerpedia* which taught direct sellers on exploring partnerships.

When habits are shared in life, at work, or in community, they create something much deeper than accountability. They create an alignment.

Think of a family rhythm with shared meals at the dinner table, quiet mornings, and weekend walks. These repeated activities are much more than routines, often we think of them as our family rituals. Repeating the regular action is bonding, not boring.

In business, the same applies. Co-founders who journal weekly, teams that reflect monthly, or accountability groups that build momentum from presence instead of pressure.

Habits don't just shape identity. They shape belonging. This is where your journey expands. This is because once you've practiced enough to sustain a habit, the next question is: Who will you share it with?

This doesn't mean forcing others to copy your systems. It means *inviting* others into a rhythm, one that grows with you both to become a shared rhythm.

I've seen this in my own life when collaborations started from one message or partnerships that grew from a simple, repeated check-in. A mutual cadence that made everything feel easier because we weren't rowing alone.

When your habits align with others, either loosely or much stronger, your motivation doubles, your resilience compounds, and all of a sudden your work becomes more joyful, not just more efficient.

This final chapter is all about connection, not control. The best habits are those you share generously. Those you build without a need of a similar return.

Whether it's a walking habit with a friend, a content rhythm with a colleague, or a morning routine with your partner; shared rhythm is shared strength.

Or take it with the view of a startup founder: You've done the solo part, now bring someone on board to move with you in the same boat.

My first name has Swedish or Norwegian roots; my wife and I travelled a lot to Scandinavian countries exploring their day to day life, their philosophies and principles.

I still remember a sentence of folk wisdom coming from that Nordic region: "Shared joy is a double joy; shared sorrow is half a sorrow."

This sentiment captures the essence of shared habits: they make the path more human. In my work with business partners, I've seen how mutual rituals like Friday wrap-ups or shared learning sessions create a sense of cohesion that goes far beyond KPIs.

Regular mutual activities reduce the feeling of loneliness. When someone shows up for the same rhythm, again and again, it builds trust – much more than discipline.

In life and in business, trust is the foundation of connection and often, of shared happiness. It builds your habits with a partnership approach in mind and enhances finding. Find accountability partners. Check their journeys for mutual connection. Build something together stronger than its individual parts based on your happy habits.

Chapter 12 Tasks

1. Identify One Shared Habit

→ Think of one habit you already have that could be shared with someone (e.g. walking, writing, meal preparation).

→ Ask: "Who could I invite into this rhythm?"

→ Reach out and suggest trying it once together.

2. Reflect on a Past Partnership

→ Recall a time when someone helped you stay on track in work, health, or life.

→ Write down what made that partnership work well.

→ What lesson can you bring into your current habits?

3. Use the "Same Boat" Check-In

→ Ask yourself weekly: "Who else is in the boat with me on this journey?"

→ Name one person you plan to support this week to float together.

→ Send them a message of encouragement or curiosity.

Expert Inspiration

As someone immersed in strategy, systems, and sustainable performance, I approached *Happy Habits* with curiosity and ended up finishing it with a highlighter in one hand and my journal in the other.

What Gunnar delivers here isn't another productivity hustle manifesto. It's something far more valuable: a humane, practical guide to designing a rhythm in life that actually reflects your own values.

I especially appreciated how the 4P Framework (Pause, Plan, Practice, Partner) invites the reader to stop and question – not just how we do things, but why.

Partnership, to me, means growing together. It's not just about collaboration, but about shared accountability, honesty, and a commitment to mutual improvement – both professionally and personally. True partnership challenges you, supports you, and brings out the best in both sides.

This is not a book about cramming more into your calendar. It's about living with intent, regaining control, and designing habits that serve you, not the other way around.

The vulnerable storytelling, especially around career disruptions, felt deeply familiar. As someone who's navigated my own professional pivots, I resonated with the idea that good habits don't begin with a burst of motivation – they begin when we choose to stop reacting and start designing.

Happy Habits isn't just a toolkit for better habits. It's a mirror, a compass, and a blueprint – sometimes all on the same page.

Highly recommended!

Frederik Böhnke
Head of Partnerships DACH at ActiveCampaign,
Published Author & Content Creator (Dublin)
www.linkedin.com/in/fbohnke

Summary

Congratulations, you made it through the fourth part about partnerships. Now you know why going together helps to turn your habits into happy habits.

Here are three key takeaways:

No one builds lasting change alone; even the strongest habits need gentle support. Real momentum comes from shared check-ins, small nudges, and knowing someone else is in rhythm with you.

Relationships thrive on repetition. Whether it's a thank-you note, a weekly message, or a habit of reconnecting: the act of showing up builds trust over time. Connection, like any practice, deepens with care.

Partnership is all about being in the same boat, paddling toward a shared horizon. When habits become rituals we share with others, they create belonging beyond seeing it as productivity. And with belonging you get happiness.

Conclusion

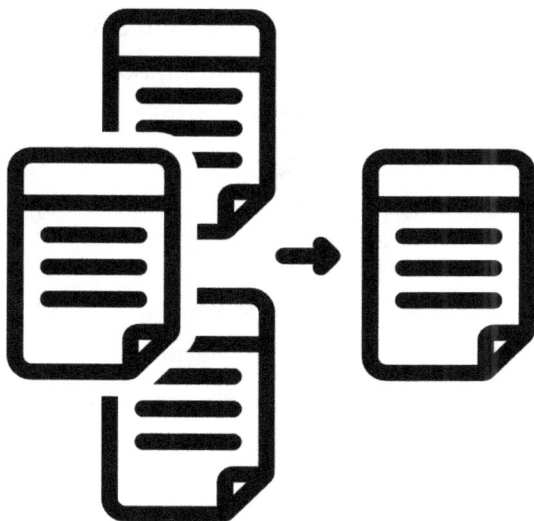

"*We are what we repeatedly do.*
Excellence, then, is not an act, but a habit."

Aristotle

One Habit at a Time

You've reached the final pages but your journey through "habitland" is not the end. Instead you're at the beginning of something better: a life you build intentionally, one habit at a time.

We began with a disruption, often something external or internal that interrupted your rhythm, but what you have done since is nothing short of transformation.

You paused with purpose. You planned with care. You practiced with rhythm and invited others on your journey which is a work to shift your identity.

If there is one thing I hope you carry forward, think about this: habits are not about being perfect. They're about being present. Consistently, gently, and with compassion, even when life gets messy and it does often in the most unexpected ways.

This book is not here to give you rules. It is here to offer rhythm and to remind you that change doesn't happen in a single breakthrough. Change happens when you show up again and again, on purpose.

You now have the tools: the 4P framework, your daily and weekly rituals, and the support structures that make habits easier to sustain. You also know that real momentum is the byproduct of meaningful effort, aligned action, and shared intention. It's not a magic pill.

So what can you do now? Start small and stay curious. Return often and build rhythms that support the version of yourself you're becoming.

If you ever fall off track, remember that you're not starting over. You're just starting again. Happy habits do that as well: they grow and grow, quietly and sustainably, together.

This book gave you a lot of thoughts and hooks to improve your own life towards more fulfilment, mindfulness, and happiness, but it requires you to take constant action.

Every little bit counts as long it contributes to building more consistency in developing good habits for your life and eliminating those who prevent your future growth.

Please don't stop here! There is more to come on the following pages with bonus elements such as workbooks, habit prompts, even an online course for those who want to dive deeper into the topic towards true transformation.

Now I'm curious to find out if the content was helpful, what resonates well with you, and where I can improve the book for future editions. Please be so kind and send me an email or reach out on LinkedIn.

If you would like to get the PDF version, please enter the keyword "Inspiration" at www.happyhabitz.com/pdf.

On your happy habits!

Gunnar Habitz
CONTENT CREATOR

The 4P Framework

Here is the summary of the whole book on one page.

THE 4P MODEL
OF HAPPY HABITS

PAUSE

The moment of disruption or reflection that calls us to reassess what matters.

PLAN

Design simple, meaningful habits that align with our values.
Starting tiny and attaching new routines to existing anchors set the stage for real momentum.

PRACTICE

Focus on repetition, rhythm, and small wins.
Building identity through consistency, even when motivation fades.

PARTNER

Cultivate accountability, support, and shared intention.
Our chances of success grow when we stop gong at a.

The 4P Model isn't just about habits. It's about creating a rhythm of growth — one decision, one action, one connection at a time.

Bonus

*"Our character is basically
a composite of our habits."*

Stephen Covey

Happy Habits Newsletter

Your habit journey doesn't end with this book; we're just getting started! That's why I created the *Happy Habits* Substack newsletter: a weekly companion to keep you inspired, consistent, and grounded.

Every Wednesday, you'll receive the *4-2-1 Habit* post: a short and practical format which consists of four insights, two simple actions, and one reflection question.

Inspired by James Clear's *3-2-1 newsletter*, this version takes it a step further by focusing on real-life application and immediate implementation. It takes less than four minutes to read and gives your week a purposeful boost.

In addition to that, *The Sunday Habits* offer a monthly deeper reflection with personal stories, lessons from my journey, and behind-the-scenes insights from writing this book.

You'll also receive exclusive resources, course updates, and thoughtful prompts to help your habits stick. Subscribe for free and let's keep the momentum going.

☞ happyhabitz.substack.com

Happy Habits Course

Want to put the ideas in this book into action with a little more structure and support? The *Happy Habits in action* course is your next step.

Designed as a **7-week online experience**, it includes short videos, downloadable tools, and weekly guidance to help you implement small changes that stick. Whether you're building a new morning routine, trying to break a pattern, or just want more clarity and calm – this course is built for real life, not perfection.

The course follows the *Happy Habits* principles and gives you space to reflect, experiment, and reset at your own pace.

This is what you'll explore:

1. Your Happy Trigger (Pause)
2. Tiny Starts, Big Wins (Plan)
3. Letting Go (Purpose)
4. Build Your Rhythm (Practice)
5. Measure What Matters (Progress)
6. Building Habits Together Stick (Partner)
7. Long -Term Habits (Preserve)

Inside the platform, you'll also find a supportive community where you can share progress, ask questions, and stay accountable.

☞ www.happyhabitz.com/course

12 Habit Prompts to Get Started

One small habit at a time – your next move starts here. Please download them as a fillable worksheet using the link below.

1. After I drink my morning coffee, I will...
    → Anchor a habit to something you already do.

2. The one habit I want to restart is...
    → Rescue a past win with no shame, just momentum.

3. I will track my habit progress by...
    → Make your progress visible to stay motivated.

4. One person I'll tell about this habit is...
    → Turn your private habit into a shared journey.

5. Instead of scrolling, I will...
    → Reclaim your attention with a purposeful swap.

6. Each Sunday, I'll review my habits by asking...
    → Reflect weekly: What worked? What didn't? What's next?

7. Before I start work, I will take two minutes to...
    → Create a micro-ritual to set your tone for the day.

8. The smallest habit I could try today is...
    → Shrink your habit until it feels impossible to fail.

9. I'll celebrate my habit win by...
    → Reinforce progress with a tiny reward or moment of joy.

10. One word to guide my habits this month is...
    → Choose a theme, such as Focus, Energy, Connect, or Calm – what's yours?

11. A habit I want to share or teach is...
    → Helping someone else improves your own habits confidence.

12. When my habit falls apart, I will...
    → Write your recovery plan now – before you ever need it.

☞ www.happyhabitz.com/habitprompts

Here is my own example of habits I developed over time:

12 HABIT PROMPTS TO GET STARTED

	Host a weekly networking meeting		Read 20 pages from a non-fiction book daily
	Begin each morning with planning your day		Block out time for focused, deep work sessions
50	Commit to writing 500 words every day		Prepare an agenda for every meeting
	Dedicate 10 minutes to deliberate LinkedIn outreach		Send a thank-you note after networking events
	Take a short walk during your lunch break		Reflect on your achievements each evening
	Read 20 pages from a non-fiction book daily		Review your weekly goals every Friday

A Window Into Happiness

Three years before moving to Australia, I stepped out of my world of deadlines, devices and digital distractions, and landed in the Kingdom of Bhutan.

Or more precisely: Alexandra and I threaded our way in. Flying into the airport of Paro is no ordinary descent; it's a threading of the needle through the Himalayan peaks, navigated only by a handful of specially certified pilots who master their craft.

As the plane curved between mountains, so close we could spot prayer flags fluttering on ridgelines, we held our breath... not out of fear, but awe. Landing in Bhutan felt like entering a hidden world, tucked away in the clouds.

Bhutan is famously known for measuring not just economic success, but emotional and cultural wellbeing. Instead of chasing the GDP like the rest of the world, they pioneered a concept called Gross National Happiness, a framework that prioritises instead sustainable development, environmental preservation, cultural values, and good governance.

This is about creating the conditions where people can live meaningful, connected, and balanced lives. This national philosophy is not a PR slogan, instead it shapes everything from education to tourism to infrastructure. You don't just visit Bhutan; you enter a value system.

We arrived as curious outsiders, greeted not just by our warm guide and steady driver, but by an entire pace of life that felt like an exhale. For nearly two weeks, we traversed the country by minivan, climbing mountains, visiting temples, and slowly loosening the grip of routine.

Bhutan has no traffic lights, but it doesn't seem to need them: the main crossing in capital city Thimphu is served by a policeman in white gloves directing traffic with such grace that replacing him with a blinking red light would feel almost sacrilegious. Actually they tried it and the people wanted to get their policeman back.

Our hotel receptionist at the Taj Hotel in Thimphu went far beyond polite service. She dressed us in the traditional Bhutanese garments for a photo session and surprised us with postage stamps that carried our own image just a few days later. Not metaphorical stamps of memory, but real Bhutanese postage stamps. Try getting that at a Hilton.

That small gesture says everything. Bhutan, I learned, doesn't just show hospitality; it embeds happiness into the tiniest of acts.

The Way is The Purpose

We visited some of the country's most sacred sites, including Punakha Dzong, a 17th-century fortress sitting at the confluence of two rivers. We crossed a long suspension bridge, and just opposite the temple grounds, we stopped for a simple picnic.

As we unwrapped our lunch, we watched a group of schoolchildren in uniforms play and chatter beside a dusty field. The scene felt like it could've taken place a hundred, or even a thousand, years ago.

And then there was Tiger's Nest, the iconic cliffside monastery that draws pilgrims and tourists alike. We rode horses part of the way (about 90 minutes up) and then continued on foot for nearly two hours. As we climbed, sweating and catching our breath in the thin mountain air, something subtle but powerful shifted in me. The monastery itself, impressive as it is, became secondary. What mattered was the climb. The effort. The process. The realisation struck me: the way is the purpose, not the destination.

This is a truth I've seen repeated in habit-building. The magic doesn't lie in the grand result, it's rather in the small, sustained steps we take to get there. Bhutan reminded me of that in the most literal, breathtaking way.

Humble Encounters, Royal Surprises

One day, while driving along a quiet mountain road, we noticed an unusual buzz near a roadside restaurant. Our guide smiled: "That is the Queen Mother opening a new restaurant today." It was no grand affair, no red carpets or barricades. Just respectful curiosity and quiet pride.

We stood at a respectful distance, watching the Queen Mother speak with locals, bless the place, and make her way back without large entourage or noisy fanfare.

It struck me how even royalty in Bhutan moved with humility. Happiness, here, didn't shout, it simply was.

Later that week, I noticed another moment of quiet grace, this time from our guide. Walking through a village, he slipped folded banknotes into the hands of several older women and men along the roadside. These were no beggars, just people who clearly didn't have much. He didn't do it for praise, and he didn't explain it. It was simply what you do when you can help.

These acts like the Queen Mother's simple presence and the guide's quiet generosity taught me that kindness can be casual, even routine. In Bhutan, happiness is often practiced, not preached.

The Day Without a Plan

Midway through our journey, we found ourselves at the Como Uma Hotel in Punakha. The quietness of the valley slowed us even more.

We made a rare decision for tourists on a fixed itinerary at this special place: we gave our guide and driver the day off. No temples, no trails, no checklist. Just us and the sound of wind brushing through prayer flags.

In a trip filled with sacred places and ancient wisdom, this was perhaps the holiest moment: letting go of structure. And in doing so, we made space for spontaneity and rest; not just for ourselves, but also for those who had served us with such care.

We even stumbled across a Swiss bakery somewhere along the way. The bread tasted like a slice of home, bridging two worlds in one bite.

Getting a Surprising Offer

Years later, after my first corporate layoff, that career shock I wrote about earlier in this book, I received an unexpected job offer. A charitable foundation approached me to lead a change management project in... Bhutan.

That job was about supporting operational transformation at a potato processing plant for a period of six to nine months. On paper, it made sense. A change management role that looks well on my CV, meaningful work, and the chance to return to a country that had touched me deeply.

But I said no. Partly because my living expenses back in Zürich wouldn't be covered. But more importantly because I didn't want to trade my memory of Bhutan for a different reality. There's something precious about a place that shows you a different way to live without asking you to assimilate into it. I was afraid that moving there as an expat would overwrite the spiritual simplicity I had found as a traveller.

I didn't want to become the guy who brings KPIs and whiteboards to a world of prayer wheels and quiet pride. Happiness is not just about following what inspires you, it's also about knowing what to preserve. And sometimes, the best way to honour a place is to let it remain a place of inspiration, not obligation.

Kuzu zangpo la

To this day, I can still pronounce Bhutan's traditional greeting: kuzu zangpo la (ཀུ་གཟུགས་བཟང་པོ་ལགས།). It doesn't just mean "hello." It means I see you, and I take the time to greet you fully. It reminds me that slowing down, just enough to say thank you or make someone smile, is one of the most powerful habits we can ever develop.

I'm still in touch with our guide. And the receptionist from the Taj? She now works in the hospitality industry in Perth. Bhutan hasn't vanished from my life; it has just taken on a different form. Like a gentle echo reminding me to pause, to look up, to breathe.

Bhutan didn't change my life in some dramatic, cinematic way. But it whispered a different rhythm into my soul. One I try to return to when I feel the world speeding up again.

And that's the quiet power of happy habits. Not the loud type that flood your calendar or chase productivity, but the grounded kind that anchor you when everything else spins.

In a world obsessed with productivity and GDP, Bhutan quietly reminded me to chase meaning, not metrics. I didn't need to live there to carry that lesson home. Sometimes the greatest gift of travel isn't a change in location; it's a shift in perspective. And Bhutan gave me just that: a deeper understanding that happiness is not a finish line, but a daily practice of presence, kindness, and alignment.

Recommendations

Lifelong learning: without a range of books and content creators my blogging journey would be impossible. That led to my online courses, webinars, and my employment at Hootsuite and most recently at ActiveCampaign.

The following resources helped me write this book.

Core Habit Books

James Clear: **Atomic Habits**, 2018. This groundbreaking book transforms life with tiny changes in behaviour to achieve remarkable results. The practical elements include habit stacking and other useful hacks.

BJ Fogg: **Tiny Habits: The Small Changes That Change Everything**, 2020. Creating happier, healthier lives can be easy, and surprisingly fun. We can change our lives for the better, one tiny habit at a time.

Charles Duhigg: **The Power of Habit: Why We Do What We Do, and How to Change**, 2012. By harnessing this new science about habits, we can transform our businesses, our communities, and our lives.

Greg McKeown: **Essentialism: The Disciplined Pursuit of Less**, 2014. Challenging 'We can have it all' and replacing 'I have to do everything' with the pursuit of 'the right thing, in the right way, at the right time'.

Further Reading

Carol Dweck: **Mindset: The New Psychology of Success**, 2006. A powerful look at how shifting from a fixed to a growth mindset can transform learning, achievement, and personal growth. It begins with what we believe is possible.

Nir Eyal: **Indistractable: How to Control Your Attention and Choose Your Life**, 2019. Learn how to overcome both internal and external triggers. A modern manual for reclaiming control in a world full of distractions.

Seth Godin: **The Practice: Shipping Creative Work**, 2020. Creativity isn't a talent, it's a practice. Godin urges us to show up regularly, trust the process, and focus on showing generosity.

Johann Hari: **Stolen Focus: Why You Can't Pay Attention and How to Think Deeply Again**, 2022. A journey into the societal and psychological factors that erode attention. Offers bold ideas to reclaim your mind.

Chip & Dan Heath: **Switch: How to Change Things When Change Is Hard**, 2010. A compelling framework for behaviour change using the "Elephant and Rider" analogy. It shows how to make lasting change at work and in life.

Donald Miller: **Building a StoryBrand**, 2017. Clarify your message by thinking like a storyteller. Miller shows how to position yourself or your business as a guide, not the hero. A fresh lens on identity through narrative structure.

Cal Newport: **Digital Minimalism: Choosing a Focused Life in a Noisy World**, 2019. A practical guide to decluttering your digital habits. Reducing screen time to make space for deeper work and meaningful connection.

Jeff Olson: **The Slight Edge: Turning Simple Disciplines into Massive Success and Happiness**, 2005. The little things we do each day compound over time. A mindset for building success through consistent, positive action.

Jaquie Scammel: **Service Habits: Small steps to strengthen the relationships with people you serve**, 2020. Transform your organisation's service culture by implement small steps until they become second nature.

Simon Sinek: **Start With Why: How Great Leaders Inspire Everyone to Take Action**, 2009. A blueprint for purposeful leadership. Inspires individuals and organisations to lead with clarity and conviction.

Lloyd Thompson: **9 Ways to Leave Your Day-to-Day Operations**, 2022. Your Director of Operations is your ticket to getting back to what you loved most about your business by eliminating daily operation overwhelm.

Rosamund & Benjamin Zander: **The Art of Possibility: Transforming Professional and Personal Life**, 2000. A blend of leadership, creativity, and philosophy. Reframes limitation into potential through joyful contributions.

Bonus Picks From my Shelf

Gunnar Habitz: **Connect & Act – Systematic Social Selling**, 2023. Build your network and LinkedIn presence, ideal for business owners and sales professionals who recognise that they were missing out too long.

Gunnar Habitz: **Social Selling for Jobseekers**, 2024. From applying for visible jobs to using clever ways in gaining a new role using the power of Social Selling to let the jobs come to you instead of chasing them.

Gunnar Habitz: **Lead Not Manage**, 2024. A modern look at self-leadership, told through a range of fictive and real stories in my world of sales and marketing, from startup to established workplace settings.

Gunnar Habitz: **LinkedIn for Startups**, 2025. My third book about LinkedIn, here for time-poor founders without marketing teams behind their success who want to leverage the power of LinkedIn.

Gunnar Habitz: **Busy Book Builder** ☕, since 2024. My first Substack publication, initially called "Writing in Cafés", provides reflections from real-world experiences in writing and publishing >28 books, >450 articles in print and >1000 blog posts, added by coffee stories.

☞ writingincafes.substack.com

About the Author

Gunnar moved to Australia in 2016 after a layoff from his corporate career in Switzerland from Consulting over Product Marketing and Business Development to Sales Management, covering the local market and later overseeing a European region spanning across 29 countries.

A born introvert, it took him a while to even consider becoming visible. Moving across four countries, he found LinkedIn to be the best way to create a personal brand and build meaningful connections. As a strategic networker and Social Selling advocate, he believes in the power of social media activities to champion the power of human connections.

Passionate about the transformation of modern workplaces to embrace new ways of collaboration, he is blogging about a variety of topics including social media, networking, leadership, sales excellence, and book publishing.

Gunnar obtained an Advanced Diploma of Leadership and Management at the Australian Institute of Management (AIM) in Sydney and received the Chartered Manager designation from the Institute of Managers and Leaders (IML) where he is mentoring the next generation of leaders. Before that, he completed his Master of Computer Science in Germany and Advanced Studies in Business Administration in his hometown of Zurich in Switzerland.

His Australian work experience began at KeepItSafe, a Managed Service Provider in the Business Continuity discipline, before creating a consulting channel for the Risk Management software vendor Noggin.

Being recognised for his Social Selling activities outside of his corporate role, he joined Hootsuite as Senior Partner & Alliance Manager for the Asia Pacific region where he enhanced their industry-standard Social Selling course by adding the missing practical side.

Facing two layoffs at Hootsuite and GoTo within one year, he returned to Hootsuite for a part-time role and finally found his home at ActiveCampaign where he manages partnerships with marketing agencies across Asia Pacific.

His regular LinkedIn Power Lab webinars include free hands-on tips around various aspects from content to conversion, helping business owners and executives transition their approach from 'collect to connect' to build meaningful, mutually fruitful relationships.

Gunnar has been featured in several podcasts and interviews highlighting the importance of relationships with a 'givers gain' approach. For the Institute of Managers and Leaders he has delivered Masterclasses about the transition from an accidental manager to an intentional leader. He has published 28 books so far including this one, most of them about travel and tourism in German.

His Australian book contributions were published in *Lessons I Learnt* about turning his own corporate layoff situation into a sustainable advantage, *Leaders of Influence* about the transition from an accidental manager to an intentional leader and *Leading Well* with a case study about curiosity being at the heart of emotional intelligence. Together with further stories, they formed the compilation book *Lead Not Manage*, released at the end of 2024.

Connecting all his experiences together, he also enjoys his role as Board Director in the historic Castlereagh Boutique Hotel in Sydney following his vision that social media should have a seat at the board table.

Connect with the author here

☞ www.gunnarhabitz.com.au, gunnar@gunnarhabitz.com.au

☞ www.linkedin.com/in/gunnarhabitz

☞ www.substack.com/@gunnarhabitz

☞ www.youtube.com/@gunnarhabitz